THE ROYAL NAVY AT PORTSMOUTH SINCE 1900

by Brian Patterson

Looking towards Gosport over No 3 Basin, 25 May 1944. To the left is the American built **LST 322**. She was returned to the US Navy in July 1946. Outside of her is the **Landing Craft Gun (Large Mk 3) 1062**. She was armed with two ex-destroyer guns for shore bombardment. In B Lock is the destroyer **Jervis**, scrapped at Troon in January 1949. The old battleship **Centurion** is in C Lock being prepared as a block ship (corncob). She was scuttled on 9 June 1944 as part of the Mulberry Harbour. In the middle of the picture along the South West Wall are the Captain class frigates **Lawford** and **Trollope** with the Repair Ship **Artifex** behind them. To the right moored in the stream is Rear-Admiral Phillip Vian's flagship **Scylla**. On 23 June she ran over a German acoustic mine off the Normandy beaches and sustained massive damage to her midship section. She was brought back to Portsmouth where she remained in her damaged state until discarded in 1950.

(NMM Neg No: N25499)

To the men and women of the
Portsmouth Command
Whose names grace the Royal Naval Memorial,
Southsea
They are, and will forever be, part of the Royal Navy at Portsmouth

First published in the United Kingdom in 2005 by Maritime Books, Lodge Hill, Liskeard, Cornwall, PL14 4EL

Author's Notes

When approached some years ago by Mike Critchley as to whether I would be interested in attempting this sort of work, I confess I was not at all enthusiastic as I did not feel that I was the right person to do it. The Royal Navy at Portsmouth encompasses a large field; it is the ethos of the Portsmouth area and I am not an author, just a good storyteller. It was the gentle prodding of Steve Bush that eventually persuaded me.

When relating the story of the Navy at Portsmouth I have used the term 'the Portsmouth Command'. This embraces all branches of the Royal Navy within the area with the exception of the Royal Marines at Eastney, which I feel is a separate story, although I will no doubt be criticised for it. I have also included civilian departments such as the Royal Dockyard, Armaments, Victualling and the Oil Fuel Depot which all fall within the Portsmouth Command.

Most of the photographic material has come from the collection of the Portsmouth Royal Dockyard Historical Trust. With the run-down of the old dockyard and the privatisation of many of its departments, many records became surplus to requirements. Some of these records were graciously donated to the Trust by the Ministry of Defence (Navy). One such collection was the Dockyard Photographic Department. Much of its material is of an industrial nature, but as with every gold mine every now and then a rich vein is discovered that any ship buff would give his back teeth for. Another source was the photographic records of **HMS Vernon**, from which the Historical Trust received a small allocation. Coupled with photographs that came from the Drawing Office and other smaller departments, this is now a valued resource although at the moment it is still uncatalogued.

The Docking Register was a log kept by the dockyard of all dry-dockings and slippings in the Dockyard, the Gunboat Yard and the Floating Docks. It has been a useful tool in cross-checking dates of photographs and at some time in the future it would make an excellent publication for the ship fanatics, of which I am one. The Dockyard's own local paper, the *Trident*, was another source of photographic material that proved invaluable in producing this work. But like all collections there are gaps, in particular the war years. Due to heavy censorship little can be found of the navy in Portsmouth during those years and consequently the Maritime Books has helped fill some of the gaps while I have filled others from my own collection.

I am grateful to Steven Courtney of the Royal Naval Museum at Portsmouth for his permission to use some images from the Museum's Wright and Logan collection. Many years ago I had the privilege of meeting Mr Wright and I still remember his stories of standing on a cold, wet and windy beach at Old Portsmouth to snap the pictures that we enjoy today. My deepest thanks go to Lorraine Carpenter of the Portsmouth Naval Base Property Trust, whose help throughout the writing of this book has been invaluable; to Peter Goodship, Lynn New, Jo Steele and members of the Portsmouth Royal Dockyard Historical Trust, and also to Steve Bush for his patience.

Where possible I have cross-checked details and dates using three different sources and on many occasions have found conflicting information. If any reader finds details of ships not as they remember them then I would ask your forgiveness for my errors.

Mention should be made of my main sources of reference which are taken from records of the Portsmouth Royal Dockyard Historical Trust collection, *Jane's Fighting Ships*, *British and Empire Warships of the Second World War* (H T Lenton) and *Conway's All the World's Fighting Ships 1947-1995*. Also *Shore Establishments of the Royal Navy* and *Ships of the Royal Navy*, both by Lieutenant Commander B. Warlow RN, have been invaluable. I would also apologise for the gaps in relating this story. There are establishments, depots and other departments of the Command that have not been mentioned mainly due to the lack of photographic material.

Finally, I must also apologise for my thoughts, for on occasions I have put my own interpretation on events. I started my working life as a Dockyard shipwright apprentice and for many years worked on warships of the Royal Navy. Coming from a family that was wholly Royal Navy one tends to get a view of things that is difficult to shake. It is for this reason that I have taken the liberty of dedicating this book to the men and women who names grace the Naval War Memorial at Southsea Common.

Photograph acknowledgements:

Acknowledgements are noted alongside each photograph. For brevity the following abbreviations have been used

NMM: National Maritime Museum
PRDHT: Portsmouth Royal Dockyard Historical Trust.
PRNM: Wright & Logan Collection, Royal Naval Museum.

The Royal Navy at Portsmouth since 1900

The Royal Navy at Portsmouth since 1900 is a celebration of 105 years of the Navy's occupation and activities at Portsmouth. Portsmouth proudly claims the title of the oldest Royal Dockyard and the Navy's oldest operational base, stretching back over 800 years.

Richard the Lionheart built a 'Doc' at Portsmouth in the same year that he granted the town of Portsmouth its first Royal Charter in 1194. The first proof that Portsmouth had a dockyard in the King's service is found in an order from King John to the Sheriff of Southampton dated 20 May 1212, ordering him to 'enclose our docks at Portsmouth with a good and strong wall for the preservation of our ships, galleys and penthouses'.

Throughout those early years Portsmouth became the bridge that connected the two halves of the kingdom, France and England, and many expeditions were dispatched, in particular during the Hundred Years War. In 1226 Henry III sent an order to Dover and 20 other places ordering all vessels to come to Portsmouth at the first fair wind ready to go into service. Were these the first STUFT ships (Ships taken up from Trade)? Of course not. The early annals of Portsmouth are littered with such notations. On 4 June 1346 Edward III sailed from Portsmouth with 32,000 men in 1,600 ships. Such a large number of ships today seems improbable but again history often tells us of up to 1,000 ships, both Royal and merchant, laying at Spithead or St Helens Roads waiting for a fair wind. Such is the sheltered nature of that historic sheet of water between Portsmouth and the Isle of Wight. Its importance has been recognised since before the Romans and today it is still a haven for mariners in a storm.

In 1495 the world's first dry dock was built at Portsmouth by order of the king and was sited not more than 100 yards from where **HMS Victory** rests today. In 1509 the king's ship **Mary Rose** was built at Portsmouth and she was not the first. The New Forest and the Forest of Bere are often described as the breeding grounds of the British Fleet. The fortunes of Portsmouth as a dockyard and naval base waxed and waned to the dictates of Parliament. But it was its geographical location in relation to Europe that gave it its importance.

1698 saw the building of the Great Stone Dock and Basin, now the oldest stone dry docking facility in the world. The 1790s saw another massive expansion of the yard and the introduction of steam. The Royal Navy had just on 684 ships and the Dockyard was the largest industrial complex in the world. In 1843 the Lords of the Admiralty considerably enlarged the Dockyard to meet the need of the growing steam navy and the new complex of dry docks, basins and workshops was opened by Queen Victoria in 1848. But by 1859 fear of the French naval programme resulted in the building of **HM Ships Warrior** and **Black Prince**. These ships were by far the largest ships in the world and only one dry dock in Portsmouth could accommodate them and only a handful in the country.

In 1864 the Admiralty was granted the necessary powers to enclose 180 acres of mud lands and part of Portsea Common to build virtually a new dockyard and a barracks to house 4,000 seamen. It was one of the largest single government contracts of its time. The millions of tons of excavated material were transported north by rail to a small mud flat called Little Whaley. This grew into Whale Island, later opening as **HMS Excellent**, the Navy's gunnery school, which transferred from the old wooden wall moored in the Harbour. Seamen at this time (1872) were accommodated in hulks known as the Naval Depot which were moored along the Dockyard wall, awaiting the building of the new barracks on the eastern side of the dockyard. Naval engineers were being trained in **HMS Marlborough**, moored in the new Repairing Basin of the dockyard, and **HMS Vernon** and later **Ariadne** became the torpedo and mining school moored near Fountain Lake.

By the 1890s the land allocated for the Seamen's Barrack had been used for other purposes and no accommodation was available other than the hulks. Ironically the Penal Reforms of the 1870s had removed convicts from the unsanitary hulks in the harbour into purpose built prisons. A solution to the problem was found in the purchase of the army's Anglesea Barracks in Queen Street which was rebuilt to meet the Navy's requirements. On 30 September 1903 4,000 Chief Petty Officers, Seamen and Stokers marched from the hulks accompanied by the bands of the Naval Depot, **HMS Excellent**, **HMS St Vincent** and the Marines, into the new barracks, cheered by the crowds that lined the route. In December of that year the first issue of **Victory** cap ribbons took place. The Wardroom situated on the opposite side of the road from the barracks had been the Garrison Hospital and was also purchased from the War Department. The naval reforms of 1859 planned to create a reserve of trained naval personnel that was to be housed in hulks within the home dockyards. This helped to foster a sense of oneness between ship-borne personnel, those on the hulks, and the Dockyard workforce. The new Naval Barracks were separated from the Dockyard and in some ways isolated shore-based naval personnel from ships and Dockyard life.

1906 saw the Signal School established in the Barracks. The origin of the school dates back to 1890 when classes in visual signalling were instructed onboard **HMS Victory**. In 1904 visual signalling transferred to **Hercules**, then alongside in the Dockyard. A separate Wireless School was set up in **HMS Vernon**, then the headquarters of Torpedo and Electrical training. It would not be until 1917 that all arms of the signalling branch came together in the Barracks. The school grew into the principal Signalling School of the Royal Navy and its experimental department undertook much of the development of all signal material. During the German bombing of the city the school moved to Leydene House near Petersfield to become known as **HMS Mercury**. In 1934 the school became responsible for the development of radar (RDF) for the Royal Navy and much pioneering work was done at Eastney Fort East (part of the Royal Marines Barracks at Eastney), Southsea Castle and Onslow Road in the city. Later all work was transferred to the Admiralty Scientific Establishment at Widley in September 1942.

In 1910 the Royal Naval School of Physical Training was established at Pitt Street. It included a large gymnasium, swimming bath, lecture rooms, changing rooms, showers and administration offices, and was said to be one of the best equipped facilities in the country. This establishment became **HMS Temeraire** in May 1971 and transferred to Burnaby Road at Portsmouth in 1988. During the First World War mining activities necessitated **HMS Vernon** using part of the War Department's facilities at Gunwharf and after the war the site was transferred to the Admiralty and became the shore establishment of **HMS Vernon**. The site closed as a naval station in April 1996.

In 1904 the Navy took over the Royal Engineers' fort at the entrance to the harbour known as Fort Blockhouse and used it as a base for the embryo submarine service. The sloop *HMS Dolphin*, built in 1882, was hulked in 1907 and became a tender to the new establishment, lending its name to the home of the navy's submarine service. Sadly it paid off on 30 September 1998 and closed the following year.

Hulks still had a useful part to play in the training of the 'Boy Artificer' and at Portsmouth four ships served in this role under the name of *HMS Fisgard*. The last was the former *HMS Sultan* of 1870 which finally served as a headquarters ship to the minesweeping squadron at Portsmouth during the war. She was sold for scrap on 13 August 1946.

The First World War saw an expansion in the Royal Naval Air Service with the opening of *HMS Daedalus* at Lee-on-the-Solent in 1917, only to be transferred to the RAF in 1918 and regained by the navy in 1939. After much good service it fell victim to defence cuts and paid off on 31 July 1996.

HMS St Vincent started life as a first rate ship-of-the-line in 1815. 1841 saw her as Flagship and training ship at Portsmouth, and in 1862 she became a Boys' Training Ship, serving until 1906 when she was paid off and sold. In 1927 *HMS St Vincent* re-commissioned as a Boys' Training Establishment in the old Forton Barracks at Gosport and was responsible for sending thousands of boys into the fleet. Sadly it closed in April 1969.

The First World War also saw an expansion of the fleet victualling facilities at Clarence Yard, the Oil Fuelling depot and the Armaments department, all on the Gosport side of the harbour. The Coastal Forces Base in Haslar Creek also opened during this period, later to become known as *HMS Hornet*, and seemed destined to have a confusing career, coming under both *Dolphin* and *Vernon* at different stages of its life, as well as being an independent command. It finally closed as a Coastal Forces Base on 31 October 1958.

During the war years the Dockyard dry-docked 1,658 vessels and refitted over 1,200 warships including 40 battleships and battlecruisers. These were indeed dramatic years for the Royal Navy and its civilian workforce, which had grown to over 23,000. On the signing of the Peace Treaty on Saturday 28 June 1919, the people celebrated in their own way but the Royal Navy at Portsmouth marked the day by firing a 101-gun salute.

With the scuttling of the German High Sea Fleet the Royal Navy found itself in the position of owning half the world's effective fighting ships of all classes and its men were well trained and hardened after four years of war. It could truly be said that Britannia ruled the waves, yet within a few years this vast superiority would be given away and parity with other powers would be accepted without a shot being fired.

In the years of peace that followed the Great War the Royal Navy continued to be the lifeblood of the city and the harbour communities. Often in those years of peace the eyes of the world would focus on Portsmouth as the Royal Navy showed its power in fleet reviews or gatherings of the Home, Atlantic and Mediterranean fleets at Spithead, to the secret envy of lesser navies.

The Second World War brought a new menace to the Royal Navy at Portsmouth in the form of the German air force. It became too dangerous to keep large important ships in the harbour and dry docks during the bombing that devastated much of Portsmouth. The Commander-in-Chief set up 'Friendly Aid Squads' made up of 1,000 seamen divided into small groups to help the dazed citizens salvage their precious belongings from the rubble. There is no doubt that the strong arms, cheerful humour and good nature of these men did much to restore the morale of the people of Portsmouth.

During this period the ships found safer havens and Portsmouth concentrated on smaller craft, but with the rapid expansion of the Royal Navy the need for more accommodation and training establishments became apparent. *HMS Collingwood* near Fareham commissioned on 10 January 1940, and many of the city's schools and hotels were taken over to serve as additional accommodation for the RN Barracks. By the end of the war establishments such as *HMS King Alfred* at Hove; the Fairmile training establishment at Cobham, Surrey; Air Stations at Worthy Down, Winchester; Eastleigh at Southampton; Ford at Arundel; Siskin and Daedalus at Gosport, and Southbanks at Bournemouth all fell within the command. The Army also handed over some of its establishments at Browndown in Gosport, Stamshaw and Tipner in Portsmouth, and Fort Southwick on Portsdown Hill.

The School for Navigation that had been set up at the old Naval Academy in the Dockyard had been damaged during the bombing and it transferred to Southwick House to become *HMS Dryad*. Even the pier at Bognor Regis came within the command. *HMS Medina* and *Manatee* were set up on the Isle of Wight to train landing craft crews, as were *HMS Northney I, II, III* and *IV* on Hayling Island, and Calshot Castle became the Combined Operations Naval Unit.

Storage of naval equipment that had previously been housed within the Dockyard now became too vast and new storage areas had to be found away from the bombing. Some of these stretched as far as the Midlands. At the height of the bombing the Commander-in-Chief's residence, the old Commissioner's House, suffered serious damage and the Commander-in-Chief, Admiral Sir William James, moved his offices to *HMS Victory* with a standby HQ in Fort Wallington near Fareham. The Admiral set his mind to visit the most far-flung outposts of his empire, no matter how small, often to the complete surprise of their residents.

The demands for Furnace Fuel Oil outstripped the storage depot at Gosport, which was a high risk target during the blitz, and consequently huge reservoirs were constructed under Portsdown Hill to fulfil the needs of a hungry fleet.

Southwick House (*HMS Dryad*) became the Headquarters for the D-Day operation and this was to have a tremendous impact on the Portsmouth Command. To cope with the additional workload an extra 29,000 billets had to be found for personnel. As more vessels assembled in the area an extra 3,000 berths and 2,300 moorings had to be found or laid in the creeks and estuary of the harbour and surrounding coastline. The armaments depot at Gosport had grown to over 800 acres employing 4,500 people. In addition to the normal wartime fleet demands for munitions they set aside 20,000 tons of ammunition for the bombarding forces of Operation Neptune, the code name for the naval part of the D-Day operation.

The Victualling Department at Clarence Yard was issuing vast amounts of bread, meat and vegetables and, incredibly, it was supplying over 20,000 tons of water daily to the growing armada. With the Mulberry harbours and other commitments storage became a major problem and an additional 1,100 separate holding sites were found within the Command, some of these sites as far away as Cumberland. In the few months before D-Day as the tempo increased 427 ships, ranging from battleships to coastal forces, received assistance in refits, boiler cleaning or armaments defects, and in the few months after D-Day over 540 vessels were repaired as a result of battle damage, grounding or stress of weather. During the whole of the Second World War the Dockyard dry docked 2,548 ships. To this must be added the thousands of vessels that were not dry docked but also received assistance by the Portsmouth Command, which will probably never see the like of these years again.

It took a number of years to transform the Portsmouth Command into its peace-time role. As hundreds of ships returned to be decommissioned and laid up pending sale, the creeks of the harbour and beaches at Gosport, Fareham, Stamshaw, Tipner and Portchester soon became overflowing with dark deserted ships. By 1947 there were over 70 warships in the reserve fleet at Portsmouth. The headquarters of this fleet was the old depot ship **HMS Resource**, moored in Fountain Lake. The maintenance of the fleet was a time-consuming duty for the 180 officers and 2,400 other rates whose responsibility it was. But the years of peace sadly never matured in the way the nations had hoped, for in 1949 Russia exploded her first atomic bomb and this, coupled with her growing submarine fleet, led to a renewed effort in anti-submarine warfare. The government increased naval expenditure, many old warships were converted to anti-submarine roles, and the fleet slowly changed in its thinking and protection in light of the atomic bomb.

Conflicts around the world from 1949 to the mid-1960s kept the Portsmouth Command busy and new developments in technology demanded a constant update of shore based training facilities. By the mid-1960s the future looked bright with the promise of a new aircraft carrier programme and the possibility of a new dry dock in the Dockyard to service them. These high hopes were dashed, for in 1968 it was announced that the government had decided to abandon the Navy's East of Suez role and to do away with fixed-wing aircraft carriers, reducing the Navy's capability almost to a NATO commitment. To the Royal Navy it was a major blow and filled the people in the Portsmouth area with a sense of foreboding, for they knew from past experience that any political decisions affecting the strength of the Royal Navy were bound to have a knock-on effect. It was a period of cuts and cut-backs which can be seen in the Dry Docking Register of the Dockyard. Between 1960 and 1970 the yard dry docked or slipped 1,990 vessels of all types, but from 1970 to 1980 this figure fell to only 1,042. The worst was yet to come. On 25 June 1981 John Nott, Secretary of State for Defence, announced to Parliament a review of the defence policy in which the axe fell heavily upon the Royal Navy. In the months that followed there were demonstrations, petitions, deputations and protest marches, but all to no avail. A sense of gloom and betrayal seemed to fill all who were connected with the Royal Navy and its support services.

However, over the horizon unseen forces were watching and making plans that would go against the nature of British people. On the morning of Friday 2 April 1982, while most in Portsmouth slept, a message informing the Prime Minister of the impending Argentine invasion of the Falkland Islands was received. By 11 o'clock the following morning, just after most of the dockyard personnel had been informed of their redundancies, they were told, 'We're sending the fleet south and it's sailing Monday morning'. The events which followed are now history and Portsmouth can be justly proud of the part it played in Operation Corporate, the code name for the Falklands conflict.

When the Fleet emerged from the mouth of Portsmouth harbour on that Monday morning into the glare of the world's media, the words of the politicians still echoed in many an ear: 'Britain would never be called on to fight a war on its own again!' How naïve, thought many an onlooker. True, the final victory brought some respite from the impending cuts, but as the years rolled by so the pruning knife was once more set to work, invariably to be followed by the words, 'We are now leaner and meaner', when in reality the service was making the best of a bad job. As more establishments closed

in the Portsmouth Command and its ships and manpower reduced, a feeling of sadness descended on many in the Portsmouth area who still thought of past glories such as fleet reviews, the time-honoured field gun runs and tattoos that were no more. Some comfort could be gained in the thought that change was necessary and if the Portsmouth Command had suffered as a result of it then it was nothing compared to other areas of the country which had completely lost the presence of the Royal Navy.

Now, in 2005, 100 years since the building of the Royal Navy's epoch-making battleship. **Dreadnought**, we eagerly await the first cutting of steel for the two new aircraft carriers which will be based in Portsmouth and will spearhead the fleet into the new century. The delays in this project are disappointing and some would argue that the sums "won't buy enough cloth for the suit". Unfortunately, the Royal Navy already seems to be paying a price for these two new giants in cuts in the numbers of destroyers and frigates from 31 to 25. Planning operations in any future unforeseen conflicts will be difficult. A Fleet Commander will have to consider carefully how much damage he can absorb before the operation becomes unacceptable through lack of escorts.

On the brighter side, in November 2004 it was reported that Admiral Sir Jonathan Band, Commander-in-Chief Fleet, cut the first steel to the second Type 45 destroyer, to be named **Dauntless**, at Vosper Thornycroft's new shipbuilding complex at Portsmouth Naval Base. This 1,200-ton bow section is about a third of the ship's length and is scheduled to leave Portsmouth in May 2006 for BAE Systems' facilities on the Clyde where the ship will be assembled. The first of the class. **Daring**, is already well advanced.

Vosper Thornycroft's new multi-million pound shipbuilding complex has brought shipbuilding back to what was the old Royal Dockyard at Portsmouth. This new complex straddles the now filled in No 13 Dry Dock and enclosed No 12 Dry Dock. In 1884 during a conference of the Institute of Civil Engineers the chairman in his closing remarks on dry docks said, "If an error has been made in the great docks at Portsmouth, then it is to err on the side of magnificence". How true, for over the years countless thousands of Royal Naval warships have used them and they have served the nation well. Yet how strange that these docks are now part of the new shipbuilding complex. Stranger still is that on 27 April 1876 Princess Louise, after launching another epoch-making battleship, **HMS Inflexible** (the first ship to be fitted with and launched by electricity), then went on to open the great Victorian extension of the dockyard and its dry docks that heralded a new chapter in the history of the Royal Navy at Portsmouth. It is as it was in another time when an old man said to me at the launching of another ship, "It's always nice to see a baby born at home, son".

The Naval Base today employs about 17,000 service personnel, private sector employees and contractors and it is said that 38,000 jobs across the community depend on the Royal Navy and spin-off defence sector industries which pump hundreds of millions of pounds into the local economy. Despite criticism of a shrinking navy and that "things ain't wot they used to be", it is still the lifeblood of the city and harbour communities. Its presence is still strong in Pompey (Portsmouth) and after hundreds of years that tradition of excellence and pride that sets the Royal Navy apart from other navies still prevails.

B.H. Patterson
Portsmouth 2005

PORTSMOUTH DOCKYARD

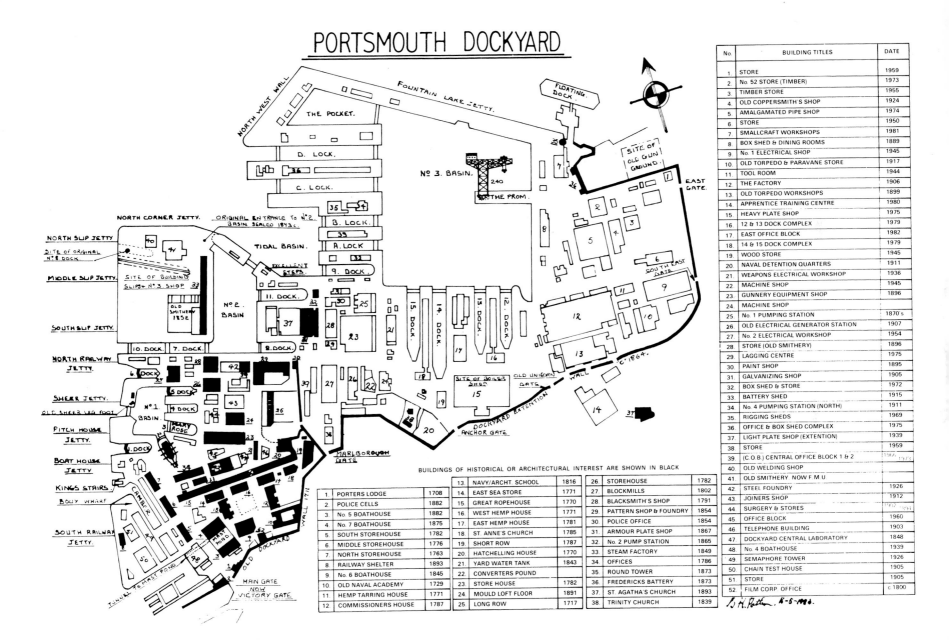

No.	BUILDING TITLES	DATE
1.	STORE	1959
2.	No. 52 STORE (TIMBER)	1973
3.	TIMBER STORE	1955
4.	OLD COPPERSMITH'S SHOP	1924
5.	AMALGAMATED PIPE SHOP	1974
6.	STORE	1950
7.	SMALLCRAFT WORKSHOPS	1981
8.	BOX SHED & DINING ROOMS	1889
9.	No. 1 ELECTRICAL SHOP	1945
10.	OLD TORPEDO & PARAVANE STORE	1917
11.	TOOL ROOM	1944
12.	THE FACTORY	1906
13.	OLD TORPEDO WORKSHOPS	1899
14.	APPRENTICE TRAINING CENTRE	1980
15.	HEAVY PLATE SHOP	1975
16.	12 & 13 DOCK COMPLEX	1979
17.	EAST OFFICE BLOCK	1982
18.	14 & 15 DOCK COMPLEX	1979
19.	WOOD STORE	1945
20.	NAVAL DETENTION QUARTERS	1911
21.	WEAPONS ELECTRICAL WORKSHOP	1936
22.	MACHINE SHOP	1945
23.	GUNNERY EQUIPMENT SHOP	1896
24.	MACHINE SHOP	1945
25.	No. 1 PUMPING STATION	1870's
26.	OLD ELECTRICAL GENERATOR STATION	1907
27.	No. 2 ELECTRICAL WORKSHOP	1954
28.	STORE (OLD SMITHERY)	1896
29.	LAGGING CENTRE	1975
30.	PAINT SHOP	1895
31.	GALVANIZING SHOP	1905
32.	BOX SHED & STORE	1972
33.	BATTERY SHED	1915
34.	No. 4 PUMPING STATION (NORTH)	1911
35.	RIGGING SHEDS	1969
36.	OFFICE & BOX SHED COMPLEX	1975
37.	LIGHT PLATE SHOP (EXTENSION)	1939
38.	STORE	1959
39.	(C O B) CENTRAL OFFICE BLOCK 1 & 2	1969 1973
40.	OLD WELDING SHOP	
41.	OLD SMITHERY. NOW F M U	
42.	STEEL FOUNDRY	1926
43.	JOINERS SHOP	1912
44.	SURGERY & STORES	1905 1961
45.	OFFICE BLOCK	1960
46.	TELEPHONE BUILDING	1903
47.	DOCKYARD CENTRAL LABORATORY	1848
48.	No. 4 BOATHOUSE	1939
49.	SEMAPHORE TOWER	1926
50.	CHAIN TEST HOUSE	1905
51.	STORE	1905
52.	FILM CORP. OFFICE	c 1800

BUILDINGS OF HISTORICAL OR ARCHITECTURAL INTEREST ARE SHOWN IN BLACK

1.	PORTERS LODGE	1708
2.	POLICE CELLS	1882
3.	No. 5 BOATHOUSE	1882
4.	No. 7 BOATHOUSE	1875
5.	SOUTH STOREHOUSE	1782
6.	MIDDLE STOREHOUSE	1776
7.	NORTH STOREHOUSE	1763
8.	RAILWAY SHELTER	1893
9.	No. 6 BOATHOUSE	1845
10.	OLD NAVAL ACADEMY	1729
11.	HEMP TARRING HOUSE	1771
12.	COMMISSIONERS HOUSE	1787

13.	NAVY/ARCHT. SCHOOL	1816
14.	EAST SEA STORE	1771
15.	GREAT ROPEHOUSE	1770
16.	WEST HEMP HOUSE	1771
17.	EAST HEMP HOUSE	1781
18.	ST. ANNE'S CHURCH	1785
19.	SHORT ROW	1787
20.	HATCHELLING HOUSE	1770
21.	YARD WATER TANK	1843
22.	CONVERTERS POUND	
23.	STORE HOUSE	1782
24.	MOULD LOFT FLOOR	1891
25.	LONG ROW	1717

26.	STOREHOUSE	1782
27.	BLOCKMILLS	1802
28.	BLACKSMITH'S SHOP	1791
29.	PATTERN SHOP & FOUNDRY	1854
30.	POLICE OFFICE	1854
31.	ARMOUR PLATE SHOP	1867
32.	No. 2 PUMP STATION	1865
33.	STEAM FACTORY	1849
34.	OFFICES	1786
35.	ROUND TOWER	1873
36.	FREDERICKS BATTERY	1873
37.	ST. AGATHA'S CHURCH	1893
38.	TRINITY CHURCH	1839

B H Potter 8-5-1986.

In 1864 the Lords of Admiralty were given the necessary Parliamentary powers for the construction of four basins, three dry docks, and two locks with provision for two more dry docks which would meet the demands of the new Warrior class battleships. The grand scheme became known as the Great Extension and involved enclosing over 180 acres of mudlands and part of Portsea common. Over 20,000,000 cubic yards of material was excavated for dry docks and basins. The picture is looking north towards Portsdown Hill in the distance c.1898. Below the hill and slightly to the right can be seen Whale Island which was formed with material from the excavations. Ships to the right in the small basin are part of the reserve fleet. Extreme left can just be seen *HMS Nelson*, the stokers' training school. Dry docked in No 9 Dock (in the foreground) is thought to be *HMS Agincourt* (1861). At this period she was a training ship (1893-1905), but was later stripped and converted to a coal hulk at sheerness (c.1903).

(PRDHT)

HMS Europa moored in the north-eastern corner of No 3 Basin c.1900. She was one of eight protected cruisers built in two groups of four under the 1895 and 1896 estimates. They were smaller versions of the Powerful class cruiser. Generally the class was criticised for its lack of heavy armament and speed. Thomson of Clydebank built ***Europa***. She was laid down on 10 January 1896 and completed on 23 November 1899 when she was engaged on trooping duties. She served throughout the First World War but was stricken in 1919 and sold at Malta in 1920. She sank in heavy weather off Corsica in January 1921 but was later raised and broken up.

(PRDHT)

The Torpedo Boat Destroyer **HMS Boxer** warped into the middle of No 3 Basin, presumably for inclining trials c.1900. **Boxer** was one of 36 TBDs ordered under the 1893-94 estimates and known as the '27 knotters'. **Boxer** proved to be the fastest of the class, reaching a speed of over 30 knots. She was built by Thornycroft. With the appearance of these craft a new breed of sailor emerged in "destroyer men". Life aboard the destroyer was an opportunity to escape the more rigorous drills and often irksome routines of the larger ships. Conditions were primitive with only an earth closet enclosed by a canvas screen between the funnels. Wash facilities were often just a bucket. The bridge was a platform around the 12-pdr gun with scant canvas screens for protection. **Boxer** was sunk by collision in the English Channel on 8 February 1918.

(*PRDHT*)

The battleship *Britannia* a few days prior to her launch on 10 December 1904. The battleship *New Zealand* (later *Zealandia*) was launched first on 4 February 1904. Later that day the keel of *Britannia* was laid on the same slipway. She was completed in September 1906. The *Britannia* and *New Zealand* were two of the eight ships that made up the King Edward VII class of battleships and cost about £1,335,975 each. With a displacement of 17,300 tons on a hull length of 454ft they were solid little ships. *Britannia* had the distinction of being the last major warship to be sunk during the First World War when on 9 November, two days before the Armistice, two torpedoes struck her from the *UB-50* off Cape Trafalgar. She remained afloat for three and a half hours before sinking.

(*PRDHT*)

HMS Dreadnought being warped into No 15 Dry Dock 1907. To the left of the picture, fitting out, is the battleship ***Bellerophon*** which had been launched on 27 July 1907. In December that year the yard laid down the battleship ***St Vincent*** and the battleship race between Great Britain and Germany gained momentum. ***Dreadnought*** was launched on 10 February 1906, only 130 days after laying the keel, and completed in December 1906. This was unprecedented and still ranks as a record in building an armoured warship. The secrecy and speed of building gave Britain a three-year lead over the rest of the world. When the Dreadnought programme ended in 1920 over £151,000,000 had been spent on 35 battleships and 13 battlecruisers. On the drawing boards were designs for 48,000 ton battleships with nine 18-inch guns. Britain's fleet was unmatched in quality and quantity and yet within a few years this crown would be given away.

(PRDHT)

HMS Nelson, the Stokers Training Ship at Fountain Lake Jetty in the dockyard c.1908. ***Nelson*** was built by Elder & Co and completed in 1881. With her sister ship ***Northampton***, they were the last British capital ships to carry their main armament broadsides and between decks. She was hulked in December 1901 to serve as a stokers training ship until sold in July 1910.
(*PRDHT*)

Portsmouth harbour c.1909 looking north from the top of No 10 Storehouse. To the lower right is South Railway Jetty. The battleship on the left, with the two white funnel bands, is thought to be **HMS Exmouth**. She appears to be alongside the coaling depot **C10**. The Royal Yacht **Victoria & Albert** can be seen in the middle of the picture moored at King Stairs and Pitch House Jetty. Above the **Victoria & Albert** is the battlecruiser, **HMS Invincible**. At the Battle of Jutland she was flagship 3rd Battlecruiser Squadron (Rear-Admiral Hood). A hit on Q turret resulted in a magazine explosion and she sank with the loss of 1,026 souls. Only two officers and three men were saved. To the right of **Invincible** is the Admiralty yacht **Enchantress** (1903). The armoured cruiser in the middle background has not been identified.

(NMM Neg No: G10370)

Haslar Creek c.1909. The Admiralty negotiated with P. J. Holland to build his patent submarine under licence in this country. By 1902 the 1st Submarine Flotilla was formed and found a home in Haslar Creek. It was not until 1906 that the *U1*, Germany's first submarine, was completed. The picture shows 33 submarines moored in Haslar Creek. Most appear to be of the A, B and C classes. It shows the remarkable organisation and development that had taken place in just a few years. Fort Blockhouse was transferred from the Royal Engineers to the Admiralty in 1904, becoming an independent command on 31 August 1912. It paid off on 30 September 1998 and finally closed on 1 April 1999. The name *Dolphin* was taken from the sloop **HMS Dolphin** of 1882 that was hulked in 1907 to act as a depot ship for submarines moored in Haslar Creek. She was sold in 1925 and sank while under tow on 19 April 1925.

(MoD/Crown Copyright)

HMS/m B11 leaving Portsmouth Harbour c.1910. The B class submarines were unusual in that they were fitted with a pair of diving planes on the conning tower for improved underwater handling although this had been tried experimentally in the ***A7***. It was not repeated in subsequent classes. These early submarines were quite modest in their displacement of 287 tons but for the crew of 15 the conditions were cramped and unsanitary in a hull length of 142ft by 13ft 7in. ***B11*** had the distinction of earning the first Victoria Cross for the Royal Navy in the First World War and the first VC for the submarine service when, on 13 December 1914, under the command of Lt Norman Holbrook, the ***B11*** penetrated the Dardanelles and sank the Turkish coast defence battleship ***Messudieh***.

(*PRDHT*)

HM/Sm D1 leaving Portsmouth Harbour, probably c.1910. She was built at Vickers (Barrow) and completed early in 1910. The D class represented a big step forward in submarine design. They were the first British submarines to use diesel engines as their propulsion unit, with twin screws giving greater manoeuvrability. They were also the first to be fitted with external ballast tanks which increased their beam to 20ft 6in. *D4* was the first British submarine to carry a gun. With a length of 164ft and displacing 550-620 tons, they were the largest submarines to date. Of the eight built, four were to become war losses. The armoured cruiser following in *D1's* wake appears to be one of the Drake class. *Drake* was torpedoed and sunk by the German U-boat *U-79* off Northern Ireland on 2 December 1917.

(*PRDHT*)

Looking down on South Railway Jetty c.1911. The Majestic class battleship moored alongside is believed to be **HMS Jupiter**. The four 12-inch guns forming her main armament were the improved wire-wound version which, with a projectile of 860 lbs, could penetrate 33 inches of iron at 1,000 yds. She survived the war and paid off in 1919. The cruiser lying in mid-stream is **HMS Skirmisher**, one of two ships. They formed part of a group of eight vessels built in pairs, each pair to a slightly different design and termed Scout Cruisers. **Skirmisher** was sold in 1920. The vessel with the gantries to the right of the picture is **C1**, the coaling depot. At this time she was the world's largest coaling hulk. She arrived in Portsmouth from her builder, Swan Hunter & Wigman Richardson yard, in June 1904. She was broken up in the Netherlands in 1964.

(*PRDHT*)

Another view of South Railway Jetty c.1911. This picture was taken at the same time as the previous picture of **HMS Jupiter**, and shows the southern half of the jetty with a London class battleship lying alongside. There were five ships that made up the class and they were ordered under the 1898-1900 Naval Estimates. Generally these were repeats of the Formidable class battleships ordered under the 1897 estimates. Their length of 432ft on a beam of 75ft seems quite small by modern impressions of battleships, but with a displacement of 16,000 tons they were tough and meaty little ships. The old wooden wall moored on the Gosport side of the Harbour is **HMS Victory**.   (*PRDHT*)

27 June 1912. The arrival of the Battleship **HMS Exmouth** - she moored alongside South Railway Jetty where the crew manned ship for three cheers to Admiral Sir Edmund Poe as he left the ship for the last time. **Exmouth** was one of the six ships of the Duncan class pre - Dreadnought battleships. She was built at Lairds between 1899 and May 1903, commissioning at Chatham in June of that year. At the time of the picture she had just returned from the Mediterranean where she had been flagship. She was sold out of service in 1920. *(PRDHT)*

HMS Monarch in the Admiralty Floating Dock at Portsmouth in late 1912. ***Monarch*** was one of the Orion class battleships (1909 estimates.) Laid down at Armstrong's on 1 April 1910 and commissioned on 27 April 1912, she served with the Grand Fleet during the Great War and was present at Jutland, where the whole class formed the 2nd Division of the 2nd Battleship Squadron. She was stricken under the Washington Treaty and used as a target from 1923 to 1925 to demonstrate how armoured strength in British battleships stood up to shellfire. Her end came on 20 January 1925 when she was attacked by aircraft in the morning, cruisers in the afternoon and later battleship gunfire. She stood up to the final test remarkably well and finally had to be dispatched by ***HMS Revenge*** using deliberate aimed fire under the glare of searchlights.

(*Author's Collection*)

Using wires and dockside capstans the battleship *King George V* is slowly warped into D Lock for access into the newly formed No 3 basin on 3 November 1914. The *King George V* was built at Portsmouth and commissioned early in November 1912 as Flagship Home Fleet. The class were a disappointment in their secondary armament of sixteen 4-inch guns. Many nations were now reverting to calibres of between 5 and 6-inch guns and were ignoring the original Dreadnought policy with regard to secondary armaments. Retention of the smaller calibre guns in the class was purely a matter of finance. The average cost for each ship was £1,960,000. The extra £170,000 required for 6-inch guns would have put them at over £2 million each. Note the camouflaging of the stem to confuse accurate ranging by the enemy.

(*PRDHT*)

To test the efficiency of the Royal Naval Reserve system, a mobilization of the reserve fleet was ordered for July 1914, and combined with a Fleet Review. On 16 July there assembled at Spithead a vast armada of 24 Dreadnoughts, 35 pre-Dreadnoughts, 18 armoured cruisers, 31 light cruisers, 78 destroyers and hundreds of smaller vessels. Forty miles of ships were drawn up in 12 long lines. A total of 640 vessels of all types were assembled. It was an unprecedented spectacle. The pre-Dreadnought nearest the camera appears to be **HMS King Edward VII** of the 3rd Battleship Squadron. She stuck a mine off Cape Wrath on 6 January 1916 at 0700. With her machinery spaces flooding and in rising winds she took a heel to starboard. Attempts to tow her failed and she finally capsized and sank at 2000 that evening.

(Author's Collection)

The Battleship ***King George V*** moored in the harbour c.1914. She was one of four ships of the class, the others being ***Ajax***, ***Audacious*** and ***Centurion***, all armed with ten 13.5-inch guns. These were an upgrade of the 12-inch gun and proved a resounding success when installed in the Orion Class Dreadnoughts of the 1909 programme. With the new gun the super-Dreadnought was born. Of the four ships of the King George V class, ***Ajax*** was sold in 1926 and ***Centurion*** was converted to a radio controlled target ship for up to 8-inch gunfire in April 1926. She was finally expended as a breakwater during the Normandy landings on 6 June 1944. ***Audacious*** was mined and sank after an internal explosion near Loch Swilly on 27 October 1914. ***King George V*** was sold in December 1926 for breaking up. All three were victims of the Washington Treaty.

(*PRDHT*)

HMS Sultan in the guise of **Fisgard**, the artificers' training ship. Laid down at Chatham on 29 February 1868, **Sultan** was present at the bombardment of Alexandria in 1882. On 6 March 1889 she grounded on an uncharted rock in the South Comino Channel, Malta, extensively damaging her bilge. During a heavy gale on 14 March she slipped off and sank. The Italian firm of Baghino and Co. salvaged her and on 27 August she was moved to Malta for temporary repairs. In December **Sultan** left for Portsmouth making the passage under her own steam at about seven knots. In 1906 she was hulked as **Fisgard IV** and started a new life as a training school for artificers' apprentices. In 1931 she became a mechanical repair ship, and from 1940 to 1945 she was moored in the Pocket of No 3 Basin in the Dockyard, acting as a depot ship for minesweepers. She was sold in 1947. (*PRDHT*)

On the night of Sunday 31 January 1915, just after 2200, a mysterious fire broke out in one of the building sheds that covered the slipways in the dockyard. Just before midnight the Mould Loft floor, the Erecting Shed and the roofs of the building slips were ablaze. Large quantities of valuable machinery, stores and two jetties on the harbour front were destroyed. Suspicion that the fire was the act of saboteurs spread throughout the area and the Admiralty offered a substantial reward for information on the matter, but nothing came of it. The building slips dated back to 1765 and the building shed to 1845. On the right of the picture can be seen the Battleship *Royal Sovereign* building on No 5 Slipway. She was launched without ceremony on 29 April 1915, completing on 14 May 1916.

(*PRDHT*)

3 May 1915. Miss R. E. B. Heath, daughter of the Admiral Superintendent, laying the keel plate of the submarine *J2* in No 13 Dry Dock. The Admiral Superintendant's other daughter, Miss M. C. Heath, had laid the keel to *J1* (seen in the background) on 26 April. Both were floated up and named by the Commander-in-Chief's stepdaughter, the Honourable Cynthia Cadogow, on 16 November 1915. Six submarines of the J class were built in response to a supposed class of German high surface speed submarines. Compared to previous submarines they were quite large at 1,210/1,760 tons displacement. At 19 knots they were the fastest submarines in the world, but were soon overtaken by the K Class with their 22 knots. All the J class were transferred to the Royal Australian Navy in 1919. *J6* was sunk in error by the Q-ship *Cyric* off Blyth on 15 October 1918.

(*PRDHT*)

The battlecruiser, **HMS Renown**, October 1916. **Renown** was completed on 20 September 1916 and shortly afterwards she visited Portsmouth. On 25 September at 2300, residents of the town were awakened by rapid but irregular gunfire from the shore batteries. Above their heads, held in the pencil beams of the garrison searchlights, was a German Zeppelin. Guns that had the range to reach it did not have the elevation and smaller guns that had the elevation did not have the range. Consequently the enemy machine dropped four bombs and then went on its way. All the bombs fell into the sea, one close to **HMS Victory** and another close to **Renown**, which helped spread the rumour, 'The Hun was after our latest battlecruiser'. It now appears the Zeppelin's visit was more by accident than planning.

(*Author's Collection*)

It was decided to use 9.2-inch guns from old battleships and cruisers to arm small monitors. In 1915 eighteen of these small vessels were built, most in just two months. Not all the 9.2-inch guns selected were of the same period and consequently their performance varied. Vessels without 9.2-inch guns were mounted with 7.5-inch and 6-inch guns. The picture shows *M26* entering Portsmouth Harbour c.1919. Her 7.5-inch gun is mounted on a deckhouse at the break of the focsle. This replaced the 6-inch gun originally mounted. Just behind the gun can be seen the rangefinder. She saw hard service at Dover and the Belgium coast. In May 1919, along with other monitors, she covered the Allies' withdrawal from northern Russia. In 1920 the Anglo-Saxon Petroleum Company (now Shell) bought *M16*, *20*, *24*, *26*, and *32* for conversion to coastal tankers. *M26* became the *Doewa* operating in the Suez area. She was finally disposed of at Suez in 1934.

(*Author's Collection*)

29

'*Peace our Reward*'. The Main Gate of the Dockyard, now known as Victory Gate, decorated to mark the official ending of the First World War. Between the wicket gate on the left and the main pillar of the gate can be seen the old pipe lighter. Smoking and the carrying of matches or combustibles were prohibited in the Dockyard but the Admiralty in its understanding ways provided a pipe lighter at each of the gates. This was a small metal box recessed into the brickwork with an iron door containing a hole big enough to admit a pipe. In the box was a gas jet maintained by the Metropolitan Police who guarded the dockyard. Thus on the way home "Jack" and the "Mateys" could have a smoke. As one old wag said, 'It was the only free fing we ever got off the Ad-mer-ality'.

(PRDHT)

The peaceful scene of Portsmouth Harbour after the First World War, viewed looking up the harbour from the Gosport side towards Portdown Hill. The three-decker sailing ship in the centre of the picture is **HMS Victory**, which helps date the scene. She was docked permanently in No 2 Dry Dock on 14 January 1922. On the right, moored alongside South Railway Jetty, is possibly the battleship *Queen Elizabeth* which at that time was Flagship Atlantic Fleet. A Ceres class light cruiser is moored alongside with what is thought to be the light cruiser *Cordelia* moored on the outside. Further up the jetty appear to be V & W destroyers, possibly *Wishart* or *Witch*. They had funnels of almost equal height, thus differing from the rest of the class. Astern of the *Victory* can be seen another of the Queen Elizabeth class battleships.
(Author's Collection)

The submarine monitor *M1* leaving harbour c.1922. In 1916 it was suggested that submarines armed with large calibre ordnance would prove useful monitors for shore bombardment, coming to the surface to fire a few rounds and disappearing into the depths again. In theory it sounded exciting but in practice the fire control system for large ordnance could not be contained within the hull of a submarine and the system failed to live up to its dreams. Four vessels were ordered, all to be armed with 12-inch guns, but only three were built. *M1* was lost with all hands off Start Point after collision with *SS Vidar* on 12 November 1925. *M2* converted to a seaplane carrier in1927. She was lost with all hands off Portland on 26 January 1932 through flooding of her hanger. *M3* was converted to a minelayer in 1927 and was sold in 1932.

(*PRDHT*)

14 September 1927. The launch of the County class cruiser **HMS London** by Lady Blades, wife of the Lord Mayor of London Sir Rowland Blades. The ship was to be launched at high tide which occurred at 1400. Consequently the unusual arrangement was made to have the launching reception before the launch. During the reception it was reported that the ship had started to creep down the slipway and that the weight of the ship was against the last two remaining dog-shores. It was with some relief that the bottle of Empire wine smashed against the bows and she slid into the waters of the harbour. **London** is best remembered for her valiant attempt to rescue **HMS Amethyst** with **Black Swan** in the Yangste River on 21 April 1949. She received 23 hits, with 70 dead and 35 wounded. She was broken up at Ward, Barrow in 1950.

(*Author's Collection*)

HMS Malaya after her first reconstruction at Portsmouth, September 1927 to February 1929, when her twin funnels were trunked. ***Malaya*** was the fifth ship of the Queen Elizabeth class battleships (1912 programme), which rank as the most successful battleships of their era. They were the first to carry 15-inch guns and the first class of battleship to be oil fired and steam at 24 knots. It was noted in the fleet the absence of large clouds of black smoke compared to the rest of the Grand Fleet. ***Malaya's*** cost of building was a gift from the Federated Malay States. In 1921 she made a courtesy visit to her donors and returned with a large black bear as a mascot which was thoroughly spoilt by the crew. Some individuals even took up bear wrestling but they always lost. During the Second World War ***Malaya*** saw much hard service, being torpedoed by ***U-81*** off Cape Verde Islands on 20 March 1941 and repaired at New York Navy Yard. She was broken up at Metal Industries Ltd, Faslane in April 1948.

(Author's Collection)

January 1934. While leaving Portsmouth for exercises with the Atlantic fleet, the battleship **HMS Nelson** ran aground on the Hamilton Bank just outside the harbour. Frantic towing by dockyard tugs failed to move her. The crew mustered on the quarterdeck in the hope that jumping up and down together would bring the bows up and release her, but this proved of no avail. A flotilla of destroyers was ordered to steam close by in the hope that its wash would release her, but this also came to nothing. Eventually with the tide at its height and more dockyard tugs pulling, the Hamilton Bank finally let her go. She was taken back to the Dockyard for de-ammunition and dry docking for a survey of possible damage. The picture shows the destroyer **HMS Dainty** steaming past **Nelson** with tugs in attendance.

(PRNM)

Unicorn Gate, the principal entrance to Portsmouth Dockyard, seen here decorated in celebration of King George's Silver Jubilee in 1935. The gateway was one of two ornamented gates that gave access through the fortifications to the town of Portsea, a satellite to the town of Portsmouth. The gateway was erected in 1779 and re-erected in its present location in 1868-69 when the town fortification was demolished and the Dockyard extended. The other gateway was Lion Gate which was built into the base of the Semaphore Tower in 1929 as the Gateway to Empire.

(*PRDHT*)

The Royal Yacht *Victoria & Albert III* steaming out of the harbour c.1935 with King George V on board. Built at Pembroke Dockyard under the provisional name *Balmoral*, she was launched on 9 May 1899 as *Victoria & Albert III* by HRH the Duke of York. She commissioned at Portsmouth on 23 July 1901. With a displacement of 5,500 tons and a length of 430ft she was impressive, especially with a speed of 20 knots. She was last used as a Royal Yacht in 1939 and became a familiar site moored south of Whale Island as an accommodation ship for the establishment. But the Royal Family never used her again. During 1954 she was moved into the Dockyard and slowly stripped of her fittings. On 1 December she made her last voyage to Faslane where she was broken up by the British Iron and Steel Corporation.

(*PRDHT*)

A peaceful scene in Portsmouth Harbour during the early 1930s. ***HMS Nelson*** is on the right of the picture moored at South Railway Jetty. The cruiser alongside is thought to be the ***Concord***, which was attached to the Signal School at Portsmouth from 1928 to 1933. To the left is an unknown R class battleship with two destroyers alongside. The outer ship is the destroyer ***Vortigern***. While on convoy escort duties on 15 March 1942 she was torpedoed and sunk off Cromer by a force of German S-boats. On the far left can be seen the battlecruiser ***Hood*** and two unknown light cruisers.

(*PRDHT*)

HMS Neptune completed on 12 February 1934 and is seen here at the 1935 Silver Jubilee Fleet Review at Spithead. Her sister ships were **Leander**, **Achilles**, **Orion**, and **Ajax**. **Neptune** was part of Force K operating from Malta, which consisted of the cruisers **Aurora** and **Penelope** and destroyers **Kandahar**, **Lance**, **Lively** and **Havock**. Just after midnight on 19 December 1941 the Force was in the vicinity of Tripoli when **Neptune** exploded a mine in her paravane. She then struck another mine, blowing off her propellers and rudder. **Aurora** and **Penelope** also struck mines but were able to reach Malta. **Neptune** then exlpoded a third mine. **Kandahar** attempted to reach the stricken cruiser but also struck a mine losing her stern. Around 0400, while drifting helplessly, **Neptune** exploded a fourth mine after which she rolled over and sank. The following day in a rising sea the destroyer **Jaguar** found the crippled **Kandahar**, rescued her crew and sent her to the bottom. Seventy-three officers and men were lost in her. Of the 794 men in **Neptune's** crew only one survived. (*David John Weller Collection*)

The Queen Elizabeth class battleship **Warspite** is seen here about to embark on sea trials following her extensive 1934-37 modernisation refit at Portsmouth. She was the first of the class to be modernised and she emerged from the £2,362,000 programme with a significantly changed profile. Gone were the old fighting tops, to be replaced by a modern enclosed tower type bridge. Machinery had been replaced by more modern turbines and boilers, the weight saved allowing for extra armour to be fitted around the machinery spaces. The main 15-inch turrets had been removed and modified, increasing their maximum elevation from 20 to 30 degrees. During her post refit full power trials the ship achieved a mean speed of 23.84 knots.

(David John Weller Collection)

Having seen service at the Battle of Jutland, by the time of this photograph in 1937, the old battleship *Iron Duke* had been relegated to the role of Gunnery Training Ship. She is seen attending the Coronation Fleet Review at Spithead. She continued in the Gunnery Training role until the outbreak of war, when she was deployed to Scapa Flow to become AA and Depot Ship. She was badly damaged by bombs and had to be beached off Lyness, but was refloated and moved to Long Hope, where she was again beached and used as a Depot Ship. She was sold as she lay to Metal Industries. By 1946 she had been refloated and towed to Faslane for scrapping, a process that was completed at Clydebank in 1948. (*David John Weller Collection*)

27 March 1937: The Modified M class destroyer *Tyrant* was what was known as a "Special". Before, and during WWI the shipbuilders Thornycroft and Yarrow were allowed to build destroyers that were loosely based on the Admiralty designs in order to achieve higher trials speeds. *Tyrant* was a Yarrows Special, launched in May 1917. Yarrows tended to achieve their increased trials speeds by fitting lighter machinery and hull construction, whereas Thornycroft opted for the increased power approach. *Tyrant* achieved 37.7 knots on trials, but the lighter construction and machinery tended to create stability problems in the Yarrow designs whereas the larger power units in the Thornycroft ships usually entailed a broader beam and therefore a higher freeboard, thus increasing stability margins. *Tyrant* was eventually sold to Cashmores of Newport for breaking up, where she arrived on 15 January 1939.

(*David John Weller Collection*)

The Admiralty Yacht *Enchantress* at Portsmouth making last minute preparations prior to escorting the Royal Yacht at the 1937 Coronation Review. Originally laid down as a sloop of the Bittern class (indeed she was originally to have been named Bittern) she was chosen as the new Admiralty Yacht and was named *Enchantress* prior to her launch in 1934. Although from the stern she appears to be all "yacht" she retained two single 4.7-inch LA guns forward and one in Q position amidships, the after structure being converted into accommodation for use by the Board of Admiralty. Were this picture in colour the reader would see a vessel with a black and white hull, white upperworks, green boot topping and a buff coloured funnel.

(David John Weller Collection)

The aircraft carrier *Courageous* began life as a 15-inch gun "light" battlecruiser, being launched in 1916. Following a Treasury directive that "nothing larger than cruisers were to be built" Fisher pushed the three large ships of this class through as cruisers. They were however, accepted with some reservations in the fleet and following experiments with sistership *Furious* as an aircraft carrier, it was decided that both *Courageous* and *Glorious* would undergo total reconstruction into full aircraft carriers. *Courageous* was taken in hand at Devonport in 1924 for a complete reconstruction and emerged six years later to begin a successful second career as an aircraft carrier. Seen here in 1937 preparing for the Coronation Fleet Review, the cruiser stern is the only tell tale sign of her former life. Sadly the Second World War had hardly started when the ship was lost a mere two years later, being torpedoed by the U-Boat *U-29* off the Irish Cost in September 1939 with the loss of 509 of her crew.

(*David John Weller Collection*)

July 1938. The Tribal class destroyer **HMS Cossack** entering harbour. Sixteen of these handsome destroyers were built in reply to certain foreign navies that were building destroyers with heavy gun armament. They were the first British destroyers in which the torpedo armament of four tubes took second place to the gun armament of four twin 4.7-inch mountings. On 16 February 1940 she boarded and released 299 captive British seamen from the German prison ship **Altmark** in Jossing Fjord, Norway with the cry '*The Navy's here!*'. She was heavily damaged at the Second Battle of Narvik and with other destroyers made a torpedo attack on the **Bismarck**. All the class saw hard service during the war, which only four survived. **HMS Cossack** was torpedoed on 23 October 1941. The torpedo struck the magazine, blowing away the fore end of the ship. She sank while under tow on 27 October 1941. *(PRNM)*

1939. **HMS/m Triton**, one of the successful T class submarines that eventually ran to 60 boats, was built by Vickers Armstrong at Barrow and completed on 9 November 1939. She had the unfortunate distinction of causing Britain's first wartime loss. On 10 September 1939, while on the surface off Obrestad, Norway, she sighted another submarine. **Triton's** Captain, Lt Commander H.P. de C. Steel, challenged the unknown submarine three times without reply. Steel ordered two torpedoes to be fired of which at least one hit. Only two survivors were plucked from those cold waters, Lt Cdr Bowerman and AB Gluckes from **HMS/m Oxley**, who had unknowingly been driven by strong tidal waters into **Triton's** patrol area. At the Court of Enquiry Steel was completely exonerated. On 28 November 1940, operating from Malta, **Triton** left for her last patrol. Nothing more was heard of her although she may have been the submarine that was attacked after sinking the freighter **Olympia** on 6 December 1940.

(PRDHT)

26 May 1944. Looking towards Fareham from the South West Wall. The single funnel ship on the left is the Heavy Repair Ship *Artifex*, originally the Passenger ship *Aurania*, completed in 1925. She was recommissioned by the Royal Navy in October 1939 as an Armed Merchant Cruiser and then converted to a repair ship in 1942. The four vessels in the middle ground are (from left) the Captain class frigate *Lawford*, fitted out as HQ Ship for Assault Group Juno 1. She was bombed and sunk by German aircraft off Courcelles on 8 June 1944. Outboard of her is another Captain class frigate, *Trollope*. She was hit by a German torpedo craft off Normandy on 6 July 1944, written off as a constructive total loss, and broken up at Troon in 1951. Next is *LST 302*, returned to the US Navy on 5 January 1946. Outboard is the dockyard Paddle Tug *Grappler*. In the foreground is a dockyard coal burning tug discharging ash and clinker into a hopper. On the extreme left can be seen the stern of *LCT 981* moored in No 2 Basin. Above *LST 302* can just be seen the old wooden walled ship *Implacable*.   (*PRDHT*)

The North Eastern corner of No 3 Basin, 25 May 1944. Left of the picture is the bow of the ex-passenger liner **Ranpura** in Dockyard hands for conversion from an Armed Merchant Cruiser to a Heavy Repair Ship. The two large submarines fitting out are the **Tireless** and **Token**, built in No 13 Dry Dock and floated out on 13 March 1943. The smaller submarine is the incomplete French craft, **Ondine**, towed to Portsmouth in 1940 just after launching to prevent her falling into German hands. The Round Tower to the right of picture was built in 1845-48 on the north eastern side of No 2 Basin and re-erected on its present site during the 1860s Victorian Extension of the Dockyard. The Large Admiralty Floating Dock is **AFD No 11**.

(*NMM Neg No: N25503*)

Another view taken from the top of the 240-ton crane in No 3 Basin on 25 May 1944, looking north over Fountain Lake at Whale Island. The two incomplete hulls of the submarines *Thor* and *Tiara* can be seen lying alongside the Armed Merchant Cruiser *Ranpura*. They were both built in No 13 Dry Dock and floated out on 18 April 1944, but were cancelled before completion and broken up. In view on the right is the 150-ton floating crane that was part of the First World War reparations from Germany. On the other side of the wall can be seen Lend/lease BYMs (British Yard Minesweeper) and MMSs (Motor Minesweeper). In Fountain Lake are Trots of LCFs (Landing Craft Flak) and LCI's (Landing Craft Infantry). To the right just above *AFD 11* is the Royal Yacht *Victoria & Albert* being used as an accommodation ship. Above her in the distance can be seen the wireless pylon of the Naval Wireless Station on Horsey Island.

(NMM Neg No: N25502)

No 14 Dry Dock pictured on 18 August 1944 showing three LCTs (Mk 4) *965*, *861* and *643*, and three other unidentified craft. The Mk 4s had a displacement of 200 tons/586 fully loaded, and an overall length of 187ft on a beam of just over 38ft. Powered by Davey Paxman 12 cylinder Diesels on twin shafts, their armament consisted of two single 20 mm AA. Their cargo load varied from six 40-ton or nine 30-ton tanks or 12 three-ton lorries. The ship's company was invariably 12 plus 36 troops. In the four months of the D-day period the Dockyard dry docked over 500 assorted landing craft, the majority with battle damage. One interesting entry into the yard's Dry Docking Register gives as 'reason for dry docking' the answer, 'Sat on Sherman tank'.

(NMM Neg No: N25640)

MTB P1602 firing a full load of torpedoes on the torpedo range at Spithead. The *P1602* was ordered on 25 August 1945 as *MTB 539* and was of an experimental design. The hull was built of aluminium alloy by Saunders-Roe, Engineering & Shipyard Ltd, Beaumaris, at a cost of £131,359. The nature of the material and new design, coupled with peacetime procedures, caused a lengthy building time and she was not accepted into the RN until 21 March 1950. In fact she became the prototype for the Dark class fast patrol boats. The aircraft carrier in the background is believed to be *HMS Formidable*. She returned to Portsmouth in November 1946, was paid off into unmaintained reserve in March 1947, and for some time was moored at Spithead. In 1953 she was towed away for scrapping at Inverkeithing.

(*PRDHT*)

July 1947. The 15-inch gun Monitor **HMS Abercrombie** pictured leaving harbour. With her sister ship **HMS Roberts**, they were the only large gun monitors built during the Second World War. They were ships of small draught for operating in shallow waters with a big punch of two 15-inch guns that proved extremely useful for bombarding beaches. After the war *Abercrombie* became a turret drill ship at Chatham and later served as accommodation ship for the Nore Reserve Fleet. She was towed from Portsmouth in 1953 for scrapping at Ward, Barrow 24 December 1954.

(*PRNM*)

On 10 October 1950 **HMS Victorious** was taken in hand at Portsmouth dockyard for modernisation that would enable her to operate the faster and heavier jet aircraft that were coming into service during the 1950s. Modernisation was expected to take three years. This was later re-assessed to four years, so that the carrier would be ready by August 1955. However, by 1953 the fitting of an eight degree angle flight deck was approved along with re-boilering and the fitting of the Type 984 radar that pushed the estimated completion date back to the middle of 1958. *Victorious* commissioned on 14 January 1958. The programme of work had cost over £20,000,000. The picture shows *Victorious* in D Lock stripped down to the hangar deck.

(PRDHT)

HMS/m Aurochs at *HMS Dolphin* in the early 1950s. *Aurochs* was one of the A class submarines ordered in 1943 with an eye on Far Eastern operation which called for a larger radius of action. The A class were designed for mass-production with construction centred on welded units. Welding of the hull considerably strengthened the hull giving them a diving depth of 500ft. Only 16 of the original 46 ordered were completed, the remainder being cancelled in 1945. The "A"s were easily recognisable with their raised bow, which was added to improve sea-keeping, and also the three tubes of the periscope standard. *Aurochs* was built by Vickers-Armstrong (Barrow) and completed on 7 February 1947. She was the only one of the class not to be streamlined. She arrived at Troon for scrapping on 7 February 1967. The wooden wall moored in the harbour is the Training Ship *Foudroyant*. (*Steve Bush Collection*)

Where did all those sailors come from? Ah! We had 'em then. 153,000 of 'em. It was the time of the Queen's Coronation Review of the Fleet in 1953 and the papers were complaining of a shrinking Navy. Lloyd's Register of Shipping recorded 5,009 British registered vessels amounting to 21,658,142 tons of shipping. Parliament noted that there had been a decline in the numbers of British registered vessels that year. What would they think now? The picture shows the Guard of Honour of **HMS Vernon** parading for Her Majesty Queen Elizabeth II onboard the dispatch vessel **HMS Surprise**, which is just passing **HMS Vernon**. The Royal Yacht **Britannia** did not commission until 14 January 1954. **Surprise**, originally a Loch class frigate that had been converted into a dispatch vessel, was hastily converted in the dockyard to convey the Queen to the review. A covered viewing platform was erected just in front of the bridge.

(Author's Collection)

HMS Chelsham, seen here in 1954, was one of over 100 Inshore Minesweepers built to operate in rivers and estuaries. All were named after villages with the suffix 'Ham' and became known as the Ham class. They were an entirely new type of vessel embodying lessons learnt during the war and experience gained in the Korean War. They were equipped to deal with contact, magnetic and acoustic mines. Generally they were of 120 tons standard displacement with an overall length of 106ft x 21ft. Two Paxman diesels gave a speed of 14 knots (9 kts for sweeping). Their complement was 15 in peacetime and 22 in war. **Chelsham** was built by Jones (Buckie) and completed on 15 July 1953, commissioning at **HMS Diligence**, Hythe on 28 July that year. From 1954 to 1956 she formed part of the 232nd M/S Squadron. From 1958 to 1959 she went into refit and was then preserved at Portsmouth for reserve at Hythe from 1959 to 1960. On 13 December 1965 she transferred to the RAF at Plymouth as **HMFA 5001**. In 1971 she returned to the Royal Navy. She was sold on 23 November 1973 to Gomba Marine Ltd.

(PRDHT)

23 May 1955. The Type 41 AA frigate, **HMS Leopard**, comes to rest after launching from No 5 slipway. Tugs bustle around to move her into dry dock for the removal of the launching cradle. She was launched by Her Royal Highness Princess Marie Louise before an appreciative audience of over 10,000 people. The Princess borrowed a coin to pay for the scissors with which to cut the launching ribbon. *Leopard* was laid down on 25 March 1953, when Mrs A. V. G. Hubback, wife of the then Admiral Superintendent, switched on an automatic welding set that joined two weldments together. This was the modern equivalent of the traditional keel laying ceremony. The aircraft carrier on the extreme right is the unfinished *Leviathan*. **HMS Leopard** was completed on 30 September 1958, serving on the South American and Far East stations, and also in the Cod War of 1975. She paid off at the end of the year and was finally sold in 1977 for breaking up the following year at Dartford.

(*Steve Bush Collection*)

HMS Victorious in 1956. The three-inch armoured flight deck is in place and work on the island structure is well advanced. The tower in the centre of the flight deck is the pedestal for the Type 984 radar that is waiting to be lifted onto the island structure. In the left hand corner of the picture can be seen the openings in the flight deck for the two 145ft long steam catapults. The skeleton structure on the port side of the lift well is the over-hang of the flight deck which, when finished, was lifted outboard to complete the full eight degree angle flight deck. Her overall length changed from 748 to 781ft and her waterline beam altered from 95ft to 103ft. Her extreme beam jumped from 112ft to 157ft. With the fitting of new boilers came a slight increase in speed: on trials she maintained 32.2 knots, giving photographers exciting bow shots of white foam and spray. *(PRDHT)*

The Reserve Fleet at Fountain Lake c.1957. On the right is the Battle class destroyer *Finisterre*, which was scrapped on 12 June 1967. The next destroyer is unknown. Outside of the three is *Trafalgar*, sold for scrapping on 8 June 1970. The Type 15 A/S frigate to the right is *Rapid*, expended as a target in 1981. Alongside her is the Type 16 A/S frigate *Tuscan*, scrapped on 26 May 1966. On the outside is *Loch Tralaig*. Astern of these ships is a group of three Algerine class Minesweepers. Nearest the camera is *Waterwitch*, scrapped at Inverkeithing on 2 September 1963. The outside ship is possibly *Jewel*, scrapped on 7 April 1967. The last group of ships in the top left hand corner starts with *Verulam*, a Type 15 A/S frigate, scrapped in 1972. Inside of her is an unknown Daring class destroyer. The Colony class cruiser is reputed to be *Jamaica*. She arrived at Dalmuir on 20 December 1960 for scrapping. The Town class cruiser on the outside is *Liverpool*, towed from Portsmouth by the tug *Welshman* for scrapping on 27 June 1958.

(*MoD/Crown Copyright*)

59

The Inshore Minehunter (IMH) **HMS Dingley** c.1958, laying off **HMS Vernon**. She was one of 14 IMHs laid down between 1951-52, known as the Ley class. Two of the class, **Foxley** and **Hattersley**, were cancelled while building. They were basically the same as the Ham class IMSs and were of composite construction, i.e. of non-magnetic metals and wood planking. They were intended to be minehunters and consequently they had no minesweeping winch or sweep gear. They could be distinguished from the Hams by their deckhouses which extended beyond the mast. Generally the class was armed with a single 40 mm Bofors gun mounted in front of the bridge. **Dingley** was built by J Samuel White and completed on 22 July 1954. During her early years (1954-60) she served as a Clearance Diving Tender to **HMS Vernon**. She was sold to H.G. Pounds of Portsmouth for breaking up in 1968. (*PRDHT*)

60

HMS/m Trenchant entering Portsmouth harbour at the end of a commission c.1959. ***Trenchant*** was completed on 26 February 1944 and operated as part of the Eastern Fleet, at first from Trincomalee. On the 23 September 1944 she sighted ***U-859*** about to enter Penang and fired three torpedoes of which one hit and sank the U-boat. ***Trenchant*** surfaced and picked up 11 survivors. Eight more were rescued by the Japanese, but 46 were lost with the boat. ***Trenchant*** went on to score more successes, the most notable being the sinking of the Japanese heavy cruiser ***Ashigara*** on 8 June 1945, which she hit with five torpedoes. She was broken up in 1963.

(Steve Bush Collection)

18 May 1960. Overlooking Fountain Lake Jetty at some of the ships of the reserve fleet moored off Whale Island. During this period this part of the jetty was still known by its old name of Asia Pontoon. The name was taken from the old wooden walled depot ship **HMS Asia** which was moored there during the 1870s. She was sold for breaking up 1906. The cruiser on the jetty is **HMS Sheffield**, the Battle class destroyer on the left is **HMS Vigo** and the third ship from the left is the Anti-submarine frigate **HMS Volage**.

(*PRDHT*)

HMS Vanguard, Britain's last battleship. Built as a single class ship, utilising the surplus 15-inch guns from the battlecruisers ***Courageous*** and ***Glorious***, ***Vanguard*** was laid down at John Brown & Co, Shipbuilder on 2 October 1941. Building was slow as other work became a priority but she was finally launched 30 November 1944 by Princess Elizabeth and commissioned on 28 March 1946. Her deep displacement was 51,420 tons on a length of 814ft. Her last journey came on 4 August 1960 when at 1030 she slipped her moorings and headed for the harbour mouth. At 1125 she veered to port and grounded at Old Portsmouth. The cable party slipped her starboard anchor but to no avail. As the tugs moved in the harbour waters turned white as they pushed and pulled to free her. By 1215 ***Vanguard*** was once more underway. It was said she grounded to pick up the ghosts of old salts that haunt Old Portsmouth. The picture shows ***Vanguard*** aground with both anchors down. She arrived five days later at Faslane in Gareloch for scrapping. *(T. Ferrers-Walker Collection)*

The launching of **HMS Nubian**, 6 September 1960. *Nubian* was one of seven vessels forming the Tribal class, formerly known as the Type 81 General Purpose Frigate. They were the first class of major warship designed to use gas turbines as part of the main propulsion system which became known as COSAG (combined steam and gas turbine). They were also the first British frigates to use a guided missile system (Seacat) as part of their main armament, although owing to delays in delivery most of the class were completed with a 40mm Bofors gun in lieu of the Seacat launcher. The whole class saw considerable detached service in the Middle East and Persian Gulf where they were said to have been made for the 'Gun-boat role'. *Tartar*, *Zulu* and *Gurkha* were sold to Indonesia, *Mohawk* was scrapped in 1982 and *Eskimo* was expended as a target in 1986. *Ashanti* followed the same fate in 1988, by which time the *Nubian* had already met her watery grave as a target in 1987.

(*PRDHT*)

HMS Dolphin October 1960, showing a mixed bag of fish. Nearest the camera, left to right, are ***HMS Trenchant***, ***USS Sailfish***, ***HMS Thermopylae***, ***USS Dogfish*** and ***HMS Talent***. In the second row are ***HMS Tireless***, ***HMNlS Zeeleeuw***, ***USS Tirante*** and ***USS Halfbeak*** and in the back row are ***USS Threadfin***, ***USS Chopper*** and ***USS Picuda***. All the American submarines and the Dutch one are of the Balao class. The ***Zeeleeuw*** was originally ***USS Hawkbill***. Alongside in the Dockyard (nearest camera) appears to be the ***USS Norfolk***, a Destroyer Leader and inboard the Command and Control Cruiser ***USS Northampton***. Astern is the aircraft carrier ***HMS Victorious***, with a Lion class cruiser astern of her.

(*PRNM*)

The old and the new.....This photograph, probably taken in 1960 shows the Type 15 frigate *Wakeful* (F159) which had been converted into a Radar and Navigation Training Ship and was running in the Portsmouth Squadron having replaced *Starling*. The Type 41 Anti-Aircraft frigate *Jaguar* (F37) was completed by Denny's on 12 December 1959 and the Type 62 Aircraft Direction frigate *Lincoln* (F99) had been completed by Fairfield's in July 1960. The inboard vessel is the destroyer *Savage* which was awaiting disposal. She had arrived at Portsmouth in December 1957 to be placed in reserve. By 1960 she was on the Disposal List and on 11 April 1962 she arrived at Newport to be broken up....Oh for the days when we had enough ships to berth four abreast!

(*T. Ferrers-Walker Collection*)

HMS Loch Ruthven c.1962. The Loch class were built to a simplified design with curvatures and sheer lines eased so that engineering firms with no shipbuilding experience or limited steel bending facilities could build small units for assembly at shipyards. Although the building time per frigate was cut the unit cost rose due to the increase in man-hours needed in the prefabrication process, a fact that was common with all prefabricated ships at this period. ***Loch Ruthven*** was built by C. Hill and Sons (Bristol), being laid down 4 January 1944 and completed 8 October 1944. She saw service in the East Indies, was modernised at Devonport between 1952 and 1953 and then sent to the 3rd Training Squadron at Londonderry. Between 1957 and 1963 she saw service in the East Indies and Persian Gulf. The picture shows her wearing the Red Arab Dhow emblem on her funnel. She finally paid off for disposal on 1 February 1966.

(Steve Bush Collection)

A fore-end view of three A/S frigate conversions from war built destroyers. The two outer ships, **Volage** and **Rapid**, are Type 15 (full conversions). The centre ship, **Orwell**, is a Type 16 (limited conversion) which left much of the old superstructure in place. The Frigate on the left is **Volage**, built by J Samuel White at Cowes, laid down on the last day of 1942 and completed on 26 May 1944. In 1946 she was a unit of the 3rd Destroyer Flotilla in the Mediterranean. On 22 October 1946 her bow was blown off by a mine in the Corfu Channel incident, which caused many casualties within the crew. She was converted by her original builders in Cowes, Isle of Wight in 1952 and ended her days not far from her birthplace when she was sold to H.G. Pounds Shipbreakers of Portsmouth in 1972. In the background lies Whale Island. Many will recognise the Wardroom, the Parade ground and the dreaded West Battery. Just above the flagpole on the left is Tipnor Peninsula with its rifle range.

(MoD/Crown Copyright)

The Ton class coastal minesweeper **HMS Appleton** makes a fine sight leaving Portsmouth during the early 1960s. *Appleton* was one of the early versions of the class that was fitted with the 12-cylinder Mirrles diesel engines. She was built by the Goole Shipbuilding Co Ltd, launched on 4 September 1952 and completed on 18 March 1954. On completion of trials she was placed in reserve. In November 1956 she became Senior Officer of the 105th Minesweeping Squadron (MSS). 1957 saw her in the 100th MSS and in March 1962 she was Senior Officer of the 9th MSS based at Bahrain. She returned to the UK in the early part of 1968 and was broken up by the Steel Co (Western) Ltd. *(PRDHT)*

HMS Grafton c.1960s. ***Grafton*** was one of 12 ships known as the Type 14 2nd Rate (Anti-Submarine Utility Type) Frigates. All were named after captains of the Napoleonic war. The Type 14s had conventional steam turbines which drove a single shaft producing 28 knots. Their A/S armament was almost equivalent to the larger Whitby Type 12 A/S Frigates, but a length of 310ft precluded a suitable gun armament. It was no doubt envisaged they would only operate in company with larger ships that would provide gun support when needed. Many of the class found employment in fishery protection and other single ship duties. ***Grafton*** was built by J Samuel White, Cowes. She was laid down on 25 February 1953 and launched on 13 September 1954, completing on 11 January 1957. She was scrapped in 1971.

(Steve Bush Collection)

1 February 1965. **HMS Triumph** leaves Portsmouth to start her first Far-Eastern tour as a heavy repair ship. Her conversion lasted over seven years but for nearly five years work stopped as other work in the dockyard took precedence. Although converted to a heavy repair ship, much of the heavy repair machinery was placed in a state of preservation and her main role became that of an escort maintenance ship which included helicopters. With the disbandment of the Far Eastern Fleet, *Triumph* returned to Portsmouth in February 1972. The following month saw her refitting at Chatham and she spent the rest of her life in maintained reserve. On 9 December 1981 she was towed out of Chatham en route for Spain to be broken up by Spanish shipbreakers. Her original pennant number was R16. This was changed to A108 on completion of her conversion. (*MoD/Crown Copyright*)

8 July 1966. *HMS Victorious* leaving Portsmouth for operations east of Suez and to relieve the aircraft carrier *HMS Eagle*. She arrived at Malta on 20 July and by 28 July she was passing the Suez Canal. During the commission she called in at Sydney Harbour, Australia for a 12-day visit on 27 October 1966. It was from there that a survivor of the Korean War, in the form of a Firefly aircraft, was purchased for the Fleet Air Arm Museum at Yeovilton and brought home. *HMS Victorious* returned to Portsmouth on 21 June 1967. No one knew then, but it was to be her last commission. She was sold in July 1968.

(*MoD/Crown Copyright*)

The Seaward Defence Boat **HMS Droxford** during the 1960s. *Droxford* was one of 20 boats known as the Ford class built in 1951-57. They were designed by W. Holt as inshore ASW craft to replace the war built Harbour Defence Launches. *Droxford* was renamed *Dee* in 1955-65 and became tender to Liverpool and Glasgow University reserve units. She ended her days as a target vessel at Milford Haven 1993.

(Michael Lennon)

The coastal minesweeper **HMS Caunton** in the 1960s. She is sporting the Red V on her funnel denoting she is one of **HMS Vernon's** M/S squadron. Her ensign staff is raked which was unusual for the class. Built by Montrose Shipyard Ltd, she was one of the early Tons fitted with Mirrlees engines. Later ships were engined with the more powerful Napier Deltic, as were many of the early Tons. Originally the Tons were to be named after insects, for example **Red Aphis**, **Green Ant**, **Golden Bee**, **Blue Aphis** etc, the colour denoting the equipment fit for each vessel. Thankfully, a more sensible solution was their naming after villages ending in 'ton' which led to many of them being adopted by the villages. This often produced 'a nice little run-ashore'. **Caunton** was launched on 20 February 1953 and completed on 2 April 1954. She spent most of her life at Portsmouth with the Vernon squadron and was sold to Metal Recoveries (Newhaven) Ltd on 24 April 1970 for breaking up.

(*David John Weller Collection*)

The Ham class inshore minesweeper *HMS Portisham* berthing in Fountain Lake, Portsmouth in the early 1960s. The *Portisham* was built by Dorset Yacht Boatbuilders during the mid-1950s. She completed for service on 26 March 1956. After trials she went into operational reserve ashore at Rosneath, in a Land Cradle. After refit in 1964 she was transferred the RNXS, Portsmouth until 1984 when she was sold out of service. The Battle class destroyer in the background is *Trafalgar*. The STAAG mountings on the after-superstructure have been replaced by twin 40mm Bofors guns and, interestingly, she still retains the single 40mm Bofors gun behind B turret. *Trafalgar* was broken up at Dalmuir in 1970. (*PRDHT*)

Brave Swordsman cutting a fine dash at Spithead c.1966. She and her sister ***Brave Borderer*** were the last operational fast patrol boats built for the Royal Navy. Both were built by Vospers Ltd, Portsmouth between 1957-60 as interchangeable Torpedo Boats and Gunboats. They were powered by three Bristol Siddeley Proteus gas turbines on three shafts giving a maximum speed of 52 knots (46 knots continuous). ***Brave Borderer*** was decommissioned on 2 April 1970 and ***Brave Swordsman*** followed later in the year. In 1979 ***Brave Swordsman*** was presented to the Haydon-Baillie Collection.

(PRDHT)

HMS Agincourt shortly after her conversion to a fleet radar picket. Four ships of the latter Battle class destroyers were selected for conversion during the late 1950s: ***Agincourt***, ***Aisne***, ***Barrosa*** and ***Corunna***. They became known as the 'Battle class AD Conversions'. Internally the ships were virtually rebuilt to give a higher standard of living and fighting efficiency. A new lattice mast that almost straddled the ships mounted the powerful Type 293 radar, and a small main mast almost amidships was said to mount 27 aerials. They had short careers after conversion owing to changing government policy and reductions in the fleet. ***Agincourt*** was paid off in 1966 and broken up in 1974.

(PRDHT)

It is always difficult to put dates to pictures, but is is likely that the coming together of all the ships in this scene probably took place in 1967. The County class destroyer *Fife* (D20) was completed in June 1966. The incomplete carrier *Leviathan* (in the drydock) remained at Portsmouth until May 1968, when she was towed to Faslane for scrapping. The carrier ahead of *Leviathan* is *Centaur*, which had been at Devonport until the end of 1966 as Accommodation Ship during *Eagle's* refit. On completion she was moved to Portsmouth to carry out the same duties for *Victorious'* (top of picture) 1967 refit, which was curtailed in November of the same year following a serious fire. Other ships present include the County class destroyer *London* in drydock and the Type 12 frigate *Rhyl* on the sea wall (top centre).

(Steve Bush Collection)

Type 61 Aircraft Detection frigate **HMS Salisbury** pictured leaving harbour sometime in the mid 1960's. She was the first vessel of the postwar naval building programme to be laid down and with the Type 41 Leopard anti-aircraft frigates show the structure of the postwar navy that was firmly built around the aircraft carrier. *Salisbury* was laid down at Devonport Dockyard on 23 January 52, launching 25 June 53 but was not completed until 27 February 57. She saw service in the West Indies, Beira patrol and was in a number of collisions during the Cod War with Icelandic vessels. Between 1980-85 she became a Harbour Training Ship at Devonport from where she was given life in 1952. On 30 September 85 she was towed out to sea and sunk as a target.

(*PRDHT*)

The Daring class destroyer **HMS Diamond**. She was built by J Brown (Clydebank), laid down on 15 March 1949, launched on 14 June 1950 and completed on 21 February 1952. *Diamond* was damaged in collision with the cruiser *Swiftsure* on 29 September 1953 when exercising in northern waters. The following day she sailed back to the Clyde at 9 knots escorted by the destroyer *Battleaxe*. In 1960 her director was replaced along with her torpedo tubes. The after Bofors was removed and the after-structure modified to mount the Seacat missile system that was never fitted. She became a Harbour Training Ship at Portsmouth in 1970. In 1981 she was sold to Medway Secondary Metals and arrived at Rainham on 12 November 1981 for scrapping. She was the last of the Royal Navy Darings to go.

(*PRDHT*)

Ouch! That hurt. **HMS Ulster**, November 1969. She was Navigation Training ship attached to **HMS Dryad**, berthed in the Tidal Basin of the Dockyard. While proceeding to sea she careered forward, ramming the caisson to No 9 Dry Dock. **HMS Eskimo** was dry docked in it at the time and it caused some alarm. The old caisson, thought to be about 90 years old, came off best and in the end there was no need for panic as it showed no signs of giving way when the 2,200 ton frigate hit it. **Ulster** went in to No 12 Dry Dock to have her bow rebuilt and was back at sea the following month. **HMS Ulster** was one of the emergency wartime built destroyers and was converted into a Type 15 anti-submarine frigate at Chatham in 1952-53. She was eventually broken up at Inverkeithing in 1981, 40 years after the laying of her keel.

(*PRDHT*)

HMS Leander, the oldest ship of the Leander class frigates, entering harbour and passing her latest sister, *HMS Bacchante*, berthed alongside South Railway Jetty on 5 December 1969. *Bacchante* had been accepted from her builders, Vickers Ltd, Higher Walker, Newcastle, on 17 October 1969. The Royal Fleet Auxiliary (RFA) Service tanker, *Olmeda* can be seen alongside the fuelling pier on the Gosport side of the harbour.

(*PRDHT*)

The Training Ship **Foudroyant** underway in the harbour, 6 November 1969. **Foudroyant** was moved from her mooring in the harbour to Fountain Lake Jetty for divers to inspect and make adjustments to her moorings. Built as **HMS Trincomalee** at Wadia shipyard, Bombay in 1817, she was cut down to a 26-gun corvette (Sixth Rate) in 1847, hulked in 1861, and later became a Boys' Training Ship. In the late 1980s she was transferred to Hartlepool where she underwent complete restoration to her original rig and where she is now on permanent display. The picture shows her being moved into Fountain Lake with the tug **Boxer** alongside and towed by the tug **Felicity**. The cruiser **Belfast** can be seen in the right of the picture.   (*PRDHT*)

11 July 1969. **HMS Victorious** makes her last voyage to the shipbreaker's yard. A Swordfish torpedo bomber of the Second World War flies overhead in salute. Saluting in the aircraft is Vice Admiral Sir Richard Janvrin who commanded the **Victorious** from 1959 to 1960 and flew his flag in her as Flag Officer Aircraft Carriers, 1964-65. **Victorious** was the first aircraft carrier to carry all three of the new British inventions, the angled deck, mirror landing light and the steam catapult. On 11 November 1967 a fire broke out in the CPO's mess said to have been caused be a faulty hot water urn, which resulted in the death of one rating. Damage to the ship was not extensive but on 23 November the Captain was informed that the ship would not recommission. However, the following day a recommissioning ceremony was held as a wake for the ship and was attended by six former captains.

(*PRDHT*)

June 1970. The Polaris missile carrying submarine **HMS Resolution** glides gently into Portsmouth Harbour for a five-day visit. She was the first Polaris submarine to visit any UK port other than the submarine base at Faslane. At the end of the visit she left for Rosyth, there to become the first Polaris submarine to undergo a refit in the Dockyard. The stern of the frigate **Salisbury** can be seen in the left hand corner of the picture and **Charybdis** on the right. The tanker on the Oiling Pier in the background is **RFA Grey Rover**. *(PRDHT)*

HMS Scimitar entering ***HMS Vernon*** on 21 Jul 1970. ***Scimitar***, ***Cutlass*** and ***Sabre*** were officially designated as fast training craft. Their design was developed from the Brave class fast patrol boats. The hull was of glued wood laminated construction and they carried no armament. They were powered by two Rolls Royce Proteus gas turbines on two shafts, and were also fitted was two Foden diesels for cruising in CODAG arrangement. All three boats were built by the Vosper Thornycroft Group, Portchester Shipyard. ***Scimitar*** was launched on 4 December 1969. She was deployed to Hong Kong in 1979-81. All three were sold in 1983.

(*PRDHT*)

HMS Grenville c.1970, following a refit into an Admiralty Surface Weapons Establishment (ASWE) trials ship. *Grenville* was converted to a Type 15 anti-submarine frigate at Chatham Dockyard in 1953-54. The full conversion of wartime-built destroyers stands as one of the most successful programmes of post-war naval construction which came at a time when the need for fast anti-submarine escorts was paramount. Although these destroyers were but a few years old by the late 1940s, technology had outstripped them and the conversion gave new life to old hulls. *Grenville* was past 42 years old when finally broken up at Queensborough in March 1983. *Grenville* and *Undaunted* were fitted with helicopter platforms over their after decks to try out the concept of using light helicopters to deliver anti-submarine attacks. No doubt some said, 'It will never catch on.'
(*PRDHT*)

HMS Sirius (Leander class Frigate) berths alongside at South Railway Jetty on 11 February 1971 after a 10-month deployment in the West Indies. As the brow was secured, the first man to go aboard was the Lord Mayor of Portsmouth, Councillor J F Blair. The *Sirius*, like her forerunner the war time anti-aircraft cruiser, was built in Portsmouth Dockyard and adopted by the City. The observant reader will notice the nicely painted bollards and capstans on the jetty. The Royal Yacht *Britannia* always berthed at South Railway Jetty to embark Her Majesty The Queen and other members of the Royal Family. Consequently the bollards and capstans were always freshly painted in black and white, unlike other jetties in the dockyard which invariably only saw a drop of paint if 'Jack' happened to be rubbing the crab-fat out of his paint brush!

(PRDHT)

1 July 1971. **HMS Artemis** was lying inside of **HMS Ocelot** at **HMS Dolphin**. A leaking valve allowed the **Artemis** to sink slowly until water entered the after torpedo hatch causing the submarine to sink by the stern, trapping three seamen in the foreward compartments. First to raise the alarm was the coxswain of the harbour launch **D11**. The 'SUBSUNK' signal immediately went out to all stations. The tug **Samson** and mooring vessels **Goldeneye** and **YC484** were called from the yard. The tug **Setter** and HL(D) **D11** kept **Ocelot** in position as it was feared that **Artemis** would push her aside and roll over. The trapped men escaped from the submarine 10 hours later using the standard escape procedure. On 6 July **Artemis** finally rose from the harbour bed. She was towed to **AFD26** at Fountain Lake by the **Samson**, where she was surveyed and made watertight. She was sold the following year to H.G. Pounds Shipbreakers of Portsmouth and broken up in 1978. The picture shows **Artemis** sinking in a mass of bubbles and white foam alongside **Ocelot**. (*PRDHT*)

July 1971. **HMS/m Warspite** enters harbour for a five-day visit. This was her last stop before going to Chatham Dockyard for an 18-month refit. She was the second of the British Valiant class nuclear fleet submarines to be built by Vickers (Shipbuilding) Ltd, Barrow-in-Furness. Laid down on 10 December 1963, she launched on 25 September 1965 and completed on 18 April 1967. At the time of writing (January 2005) the decommissioned **Warspite**, along with **Splendid**, **Courageous**, **Conqueror** and **Valiant**, are laid up in long-term storage at Plymouth.

(*PRDHT*)

September 1971. **HMS Belfast** leaving Portsmouth to take up her new role as a museum ship in the Pool of London. She ended her service life moored in No 3 Basin on the North Wall as headquarters ship of the Reserve Fleet at Portsmouth (**HMS Bellerophon**). In March 1971 she flew a symbolic paying-off pennant to mark the end of her career, which also marked the end of **HMS Bellerophon** at Portsmouth when the Reserve Fleet organisation moved to Chatham. **Belfast** was officially handed over to the HMS Belfast Trust on Trafalgar Day 1971. Although no longer one of Her Majesty's Ships, special permission was granted for her to wear the White Ensign. As *The Times* put it, "The Navy Waives the Rules". *(PRDHT)*

Two generations of Anti-submarine frigate are seen together in 1971. The inboard ship is the Type 15 frigate *Ulster*, converted from a WWII destroyer to fill a gap in modern ASW tonnage following the start of the Cold War. *Dundas* (F48) was a Type 14 frigate, designed as a cheap, easy-build and effective ASW vessel, to complement the more sophisticated and expensive, Type 12s which were entering service. Single shaft vessels whose main armament was two Limbo A/S mortars, these rather utilitarian vessels too lightly constructed to cope with the rough seas and high speeds encountered during modern ASW operations. In fact during the late 1950s their hulls were strengthened to allow them to operate off Iceland in the Fishery Protection role. Further, the third 40mm gun mounted on the quarterdeck had to be removed after hull cracking was discovered in some vessels. *Dundas* was broken up at Troon in 1983 and *Ulster* at Inverkeithing in 1980.

(David John Weller Collection)

HMS Mermaid, probably April 1972 when she was purchased by the British government and transferred to the Royal Navy at Portsmouth. She was originally built for the Republic of Ghana as a Presidential Yacht to be named ***Black Swan***. When President Nkrumah was deposed the new government cancelled the contract with Yarrow Shipbuilding Ltd. Yarrow completed the vessel in 1968 in the hope of finding a buyer. Her weaponry was not up to the standard of Royal Navy vessels and it proved difficult finding a role for her in the fleet. In 1976 she was in collision with the minesweeper ***HMS Fittleton*** while exercising in the English Channel. ***Fittleton*** sank with the loss of 12 of her RNVR crew. In April 1977 ***Mermaid*** was transferred to the Malaysian Navy and renamed ***HangTuah***.

(*PRDHT*)

*HMS **Bulwark*** passing her sister ship ***Albion*** in refit. The date of the picture is unknown but thought to be 1972 when both carriers were in Portsmouth. It would appear that ***Bulwark*** is having a families' day at sea from the number of civilians on her flight deck. It was from ***Bulwark*** that the first live television transmission from a Royal Navy ship at sea was made in 1955. ***HMS Albion*** was the first British carrier completed with an angled flight deck. She finally decommissioned on 2 March 1973 and was sold to Wilson Walker Engineering. On 16 November 1973 she was towed to Faslane to be broken up for scrap.

(PRDHT)

HMS Blake was one of three ships known as the Tiger class cruisers. They were the last of the war-built cruisers to be launched: others of the class were broken up on the slipways or cancelled before they were laid down in 1946. Work on the three ships resumed in 1955 to a different design centred on the new rapid firing 6-inch and 3-inch guns. **Blake** was convert-ed to a command helicopter cruiser at Portsmouth Dockyard early in 1965 until re-commissioned on 23 April 1969. She was broken up at Shipbreaking (Queenborough) Ltd, Cairnryan 1982. She was the last cruiser in commission in the Royal Navy, ending almost 100 years of the cruiser tradition. Of her two sisters, **Tiger** was broken up in Spain in 1986 and **Lion** was broken up by Ward, Inverkeithing in 1975. Unlike her sisters, **Lion** was not converted to a helicopter command ship.

(David John Weller Collection)

HMS Eagle at South Railway Jetty, 1972. She was one of four ships ordered in 1942 as improved Implacable class aircraft carriers, the others being **Audacious**, **Ark Royal** and **Africa**. In 1945 the **Eagle** and **Africa** were cancelled. **Audacious** was the most advanced in building and was renamed **Eagle** in January 1946. She completed in January 1951 and was extensively rebuilt at Devonport Dockyard in 1959-64, when her deep displacement rose to 50,553 tons. She arrived in Portsmouth on 26 January 1972 to pay off for disposal and was moved to Middle Slip Jetty, where the Royal Engineers built a roadway from her flight deck to the jetty to aid de-storing. On 6 August 1972 she was towed to Plymouth to spend the next six years of her life being cannibalised to support her sister, **Ark Royal**. In October 1978 she was finally towed away to the shipbreaker's yard on the Clyde. *(MoD/Crown Copyright)*

Looking South across Fountain Lake and over No 3 Basin in July 1972. On the right is the stern of **London** with the cruiser **Blake** astern of her. Alongside **Blake** is **Oilwell**, and on the outside is a PAS craft and **Landing Barge Kitchen No 6** (LBK6) on the inside, possibly the only vessel still in MoD use that was used during the Normandy landings. LBKs were swim barges of 150 tons with a crew of 25 and stores to feed 900 men for one week. They were subsequently used as floating galleys for ships in refit. Astern of **Blake** is **Kent** with the Tank Cleaning Vessel **Lundy** and minesweeper **Shoulton** alongside. On the inner wall is **Barrosa** and an unknown sister. On the Promontory with the 240 ton crane is **Corunna** alongside a DLG, with a Leander and another DLG on the South side of the wall. On the far side of the Basin in Dry Dock No 12 on the left is **Mermaid**. At this time she still had no name and was known as Ex-Ghana frigate. In No 13 Dock is **Ashanti** with possibly **Leopard** on the wall. On the right in No 15 Dry Dock is **Endurance** undergoing refit.

(*PRDHT*)

The midget submarine *X24* arrived in the Dockyard during the early part of 1973 for a refit. *X24* was ordered with six other boats on 20 July 1942 and built by Marshall (Gainsborough) in 1944. She was hulked at Portsmouth in 1945. For many years she rested on blocks at the Royal Navy's submarine headquarters, *HMS Dolphin*, where time took its toll. Plans were considered to display the boat close to *HMS Victory* in the Dockyard with part of the hull cut away for visitor viewing. The refit work package involved renewing the casing and repairs to the keel, rudder and hydroplanes. The rest of the plan never materialised, and she is now exhibited in the Royal Navy Submarine Museum at Gosport.

(*PRDHT*)

Overlooking the south-western corner of No 3 Basin, May 1974. In the bottom of the picture, in C Lock is the destroyer *Norfolk* with the Royal Yacht *Britannia* in A Lock. The Leander class frigate *Aurora* is seen alongside the Type 15 anti-submarine frigate *Undaunted* moored in the Tidal Basin. Above them in No 8 Dry Dock can just be seen the funnel and bridge of the tug *Cyclone* which was docked down with PAS craft No 150. On the left of the picture is the Leander class frigate *Hermione* with the cruiser *Blake* in No 14 Dry Dock and *London* in No 15 Dry Dock.

(PRDHT)

The Submarine rescue and diving vessel **HMS Reclaim**, moored on the north wall of the Tidal Basin in August 1975. **Reclaim** was one of the King Salvor class ocean salvage vessels built by W. Simons (Renfrew) under the name **Salverdant**. She was converted while building and completed in October 1948 as a submarine rescue and diving vessel under the name **Reclaim**. For most of her service she operated from **HMS Vernon**. She carried out the first experiments in underwater television and used it to locate the missing submarine **HMS Affray**, lost in the English Channel with all hands on 17 April 1951. She was sold to a Belgian shipbreaker in 1982 and was scrapped at Bruges.

(*PRDHT*)

In 1975 the newly completed Type 42 destroyer **Sheffield** is joined on her berth by the last WWII destroyer in commission, the Battleclass **Matapan**. Although **Matapan** is heavily modified, the differnece in hull size is quite apparent, with the modern destroyer appearing to be significantly broader than her WWII counterpart. **Sheffield** was the first of the Type 42 class and was completed in February 1975. Designed to provide the fleet with Air-defence following the demise of the fixed wing carrier in the RN, the first of the class were a bit of a compromise. The treasury imposed a strict cash limit on each ship, which resulted in a foreshortened vessel, a smaller warload of missiles and the old generation Type 965 radar. Subsequent batches received the newer Type 1022 radar (subsequently backfitted on the older ships) and the last four were completed to the original long hull design. Sheffield was lost during the Falklands War following an Exocet hit on 4 May 1982.. As fires raged out of control the ship was abandoned and taken in tow, but she sank on 10 May. *(David John Weller Collection)*

Far left: On 11 March 1976 **HMS Falmouth** arrived at Portsmouth from her third Cod War patrol with damage sustained in collision with the Icelandic gunboat *Tyr*. *Falmouth* berthed in the Tidal Basin where the Dockyard diving boat and diving team (seen in the left hand corner of the picture), were brought alongside for divers to survey the underwater section of the bow and cut away damaged plating that would interfere with dry docking. (PRDHT)

Left: On 21 May *Falmouth* was dry docked in D Lock for a thorough survey and to remove her damaged structure. The ship was taken out of the lock on 9 June to await the construction of a new bow in the yard's heavy plate shop. The picture shows *Falmouth* in No 15 Dry Dock with the damaged structure removed. A cradle, into which the new bow section was lowered and slid across into position on the ship for fitting, can be seen in the lower left of the picture. *(PRDHT)*

Right: *Falmouth* entered No 15 Dry Dock on 15 July 1976. Work on the new bow continued throughout August, and at the same time other damage sustained during the collision was put right, together with operational defects. All work was finished a week ahead of schedule and *Falmouth* un-docked on 3 September 1976. As one of her officers said, 'You couldn't even see the join.' The picture was taken the day before undocking. *(PRDHT)*

A busy scene in the harbour as tugs manoeuvre **HMS Hermes**, possibly into one of the Locks. The paddle tug is **Forceful** assisted by two Dog class tugs. The fleet tender **Beaulieu** appears to be just passing by. Also in the picture are two dockyard launches, **D17** and **D50**. The black-hulled ship ahead of **Hermes** appears to be an old weather ship, possibly one of the Castle class frigate conversions. The date of the picture is not known but thought to be in the mid-1970s.

(PRDHT)

November 1977. The Fast Patrol Boat **HMS Cutlass** is gently eased under the new Haslar Bridge and between the remains of the old one as she leaves Haslar Gunboat Yard after completing a 12-week refit. People who worked at Haslar, Dolphin, the Gunboat Yard and the experimental tanks often referred to Haslar bridge as 'Pneumonia Bridge'. Its exposed position in winter-time was something to be dreaded.

(*PRDHT*)

The Silver Jubilee Review of the Fleet, 28 June 1977. The Royal Yacht *Britannia* enters the Review Lines preceded by the Trinity House Vessel *Patricia* and escorted by the destroyer *Birmingham*. Nearest the camera are the aircraft carriers *Ark Royal* and *Hermes* followed by *Fearless*, *Tiger*, *Glamorgan*, *Fife* and *Kent*. HM submarines are *Valiant*, *Churchill*, *Dreadnought*, *Oracle*, *Cachalot*, *Walrus*, *Sealion*, *Osiris*, *Orpheus*, *Opossum*, *Ocelot* and in the distance *Opportune*.

(*MoD/Crown Copyright*)

An aerial view of **HMS Vernon** during the Silver Jubilee year, 1977. An inscription to mark **Vernon's** own anniversary can be seen around the edge of the heli-pad. The United Services sport field is in the top of the picture. The city's power station is the building in the top right hand corner. No doubt many on old Vernon will recognise some of the buildings. The whole of this site has now been redeveloped into a shopping and entertainment complex.

(*PRDHT*)

HMS Matapan as she appeared on completion of her reconstruction to a sonar trials ship. Work started in January 1970, docking down in No 14 Dry Dock on a 13ft high plinth. This unusual arrangement was necessary to construct the deep skeg on the bottom of the ship. As work progressed so the plinth was cut away, transferring the weight of the ship to a new bottom line several feet below her docking line. Coming out of dry dock on 1 November 1971, her displacement had risen from 1,775 tons to 3,835 tons and her draught from 8ft 6in to 22ft. Her rebuild also involved providing workshops and additional accommodation for scientists, some of whom were women. She commissioned at Portsmouth on 2 February 1973. **Matapan** was broken up between 1979-80 at Blyth.

(*PRDHT*)

Dockyard Harbour Launch *D23* crossing the harbour. These popular little craft were a familiar sight in almost all dockyards and naval bases around the world. Their origin can be traced back to the early days of the steam pinnace of the late 1870s. They performed all the small towing duties in the basins and docks and were invaluable in ferrying passengers to ships moored in the creeks, trots or other establishments. They were originally known as HSLs (Harbour Service Launches), but on 13 August 1942, CAFO No 1518 stated that the abbreviation HSL created confusion as the term was also applied to High Speed Launches of the RAF. In future steam-driven craft were to be abbreviated as HL(S) and diesel-driven craft as HL(D). The last three in Portsmouths Dockyard's service, *D49*, *6507* and *6510*, were disposed of in 1996.   (*PRDHT*)

HMS Orkney photographed from ***HMS Dolphin*** as she left harbour June 1979. ***Orkney*** was one of a class of seven vessels designated Offshore Patrol Craft. Orders for the first five were announced in 1975 and the last two, ***Anglesey*** and ***Alderney***, were ordered in 1977. They had to be fitted with enlarged bilge keels to dampen down their rolling motion, which was said to be uncomfortable in bad weather, and the last two of the class were fitted with stabilisers. All were built by Hall Russell & Co Ltd. ***Orkney*** was launched on 29 June 1976 and commissioned on 25 February 1977. The building cost for ***Orkney*** was £3.3 million. She was deleted in 1999.

(*PRDHT*)

The escort maintenance ship **Rame Head** moored off Whale Island in Fountain Lake, 1979. She is one of the few examples still afloat of the standard cargo ships that were built in large numbers during the Second World War. She was laid down at North Vancouver Ship Repairers (Canada) 12 July 1944 and launched on 22 November 1944. She commissioned after 13 months' building time on 18 August 1945. **Rame Head** was modernised in 1960-62 and became an accommodation ship at Portsmouth in 1976. At the time of writing (2005) she is moored in Fareham Lake and described as a Royal Marine training ship.

(MoD/Crown Copyright)

HMS Vernon 1981. ***Vernon*** was the Torpedo School established in hulks at Portsmouth Harbour in 1876. It took over the army's Gunwharf establishment on 1 October 1923 for the Navy's Mining and Torpedo School. It paid off on 31 March 1986, although it was still used for other purposes until finally closed on 1 April 1996. On the left of the picture are MCMV's ***Ledbury***, and behind the crane an unknown Ton class sweeper with the Jetfoil ***Speedy*** (sold 1986) on the outside. Ahead is the minehunter ***Iveston*** with what is thought to be the survey vessel ***Woodlark*** (ex-***Yaxham***) in front. She was expended as a target in 1986. The Hunter alongside the wall is ***Hubberston***. The vessel outside is not known, but the VT2 Hovercraft on the outside was attached to the Royal Navy Hovercraft Trials Unit at Lee-on-the-Solent which closed in Autum1982.

(*PRDHT*)

News of the invasion of the Falkland Islands broke on the morning of Friday 2 April 1982. It was a side issue to Dockyard personnel, whose fate was decided at 1000 that day when they were informed of redundancies in the wake of the 1981 Defence Review. By 1100 they were told 'We're sending the fleet south'. *Hermes* was in the second week of her maintainace programme with her superstructure festooned in staging and machinery under refit. *Intrepid* was paid off and de-stored for possible sale. *Stromness* had been decommissioned and was also up for sale. *Invincible's* crew was on Easter leave and the ship was having operational defects put right. After a magnificent effort by all concerned, *Hermes* and *Invincible* sailed on the following Monday morning, 5 April. The picture shows *Hermes* leaving Portsmouth to go to war.
(*PRDHT*)

The huge mass of the **Baltic Ferry** moored in C Lock while fitting out for the Falklands War. She sailed on 9 May in company with **Nordic Ferry** carrying a Merchant Navy crew of 43, a naval party of 14 and 105 army personnel as well as hundreds of tons of military stores and helicopters. By now the Falklands War had become known as 'Operation Corporate' the overall code-name to recover the Falkland Islands.

(*PRDHT*)

25 April 1982. The 12,998 ton P&O 'Ro-Ro' Ferry **Norland** leaving for the South Atlantic with the Second Parachute Regiment on board. The Dockyard had only 28 hours' notice before she arrived and conversion work began. She was in hand for only 82 hours (3.5 days) during which it was said that 320 man-weeks of work were completed. This involved fitting two helicopter pads with tie-down points, fresh water-making plants, communication fitment, additional navigation equipment, re-fuelling at sea arrangements, battery charging facilities and accommodation for troops. Incredibly, all this was completed while the ship was being stored and embarking troops.　　　(*PRDHT*)

RMS St Helena leaving for the South Atlantic after being in the Dockyard for just over 17 days for conversion to a minehunter support ship. It was assumed that commercial shipyards would be able to convert and load commercial shipping for Operation Corporate, but the sheer volume of work and the skill facilities required in such a short time span soon swamped available resources. In the end, although commercial shipyards played a crucial part, the majority of the work fell to the two Royal Dockyards of Portsmouth and Devonport with Rosyth and Gibraltar also playing a part.

(PRDHT)

10 July 1982. The crew of the United States destroyer **Charles F. Adams** salute as **HMS Glamorgan** passes her on South Railway Jetty on her way up the harbour after returning from the South Atlantic. Her starboard side shows no sign of the damage sustained by the Excocet missile that struck her and exploded in the ship's hangar on the morning of 12 June 1982, 17 miles south-west of Port Stanley. Fire penetrated to the galley and machinery spaces below decks, but good damage control and efficient fire fighting saved the ship. Thirteen of her brave crew were lost in the attack and 15 were wounded.

(PRDHT)

21 July 1982. **HMS Hermes** comes home from the Falklands War to a hero's welcome. Her weather-beaten hull said much for the conditions experienced in those cold southern seas. Since leaving Portsmouth on 5 April she had spent 108 days continually at sea, travelling over 35,000 miles.

(*PRDHT*)

Another rousing welcome, this time for the destroyer **Cardiff** returning from the South Atlantic. In the foreground personnel of **HMS Vernon** raise caps for three cheers. **Cardiff** has the distinction of the last successful missile engagement by a warship in the campaign with the destruction of an Argentine Canberra bomber late on 13 June 1982. *(PRDHT)*

HMS *Illustrious* heads south for the Falklands and passes ***Hermes***. In the background can be seen ***Bulwark***. ***Illustrious*** relieved ***Invincible*** on 27 August 1982, allowing her and the ***Bristol*** to return to Portsmouth. ***Illustrious*** was completed months ahead of schedule date, thanks to the splendid efforts of her builders Swan Hunters of Tyneside, and the work of the Royal Dockyards. ***Illustrious*** stayed in the Falklands area until 21 October, four days after the first of the RAF's Phantoms arrived at Port Stanley to assume responsibility for the air defence of the islands.

(*PRDHT*)

17 September 1982. Amid all the cheering and confusion of small boats, tugs gently push *Invincible* onto the wall on her return from the Falklands War. Her Majesty the Queen and Prince Philip were amongst those waiting on the dockside. The aerial platforms were brought in by TV companies who were determined to catch every tear that fell. Even so, nothing could take away the tremendous pleasure felt by all on seeing their loved ones step ashore to be presented with a red rose. At the same time *Bristol* followed *Invincible* into harbour and although her crew received an equally warm welcome by their loved ones, the TV spotlight fell on *Invincible*.

(*PRDHT*)

HMS Sentinel passing the Hot Walls at Old Portsmouth on her way into harbour. ***Sentinel*** was originally named ***Seaforth Warrior***, owned by Zellandrame Ltd and managed by Seaforth Marine. She was acquired by the MoD in February 1983 and commissioned into the Royal Navy on 14 January 1984 for Falkland Islands patrol duties. She is 198ft overall with a beam of 45.5ft, a speed of 14 knots and a compliment of 26.

(MoD/Crown Copyright)

August 1984. A view of the Oiling Pier at the Gosport Oil Fuel Department. One of the Ol class Fleet tankers is moored on the inside of **Pearleaf** (A77). To the right are two of the smaller fleet tankers, **Grey Rover** and possibly **Blue Rover**. The Oil Fuel Department at Gosport was one of the first in the naval service with storage tanks planned as early as 1910. Just before the Second World War the Fuel Department was enlarged by building tanks under Portsdown Hill at the north of the harbour. With a shrinking fleet these are now believed to have been de-activated.

(*PRDHT*)

10 November 1984. To help with the problem of water-borne transport around the Falkland Islands it was decided to send tenders from UK dockyards. The Danish *MV Edel Scheel* was hired and sailed for the Falklands with a deck cargo of three small craft: *RMAS Blankeney* which been had sailed from Rosyth to Portsmouth by her own crew, the Portsmouth-based fleet tender *Beaulieu*, and a 52ft passenger launch. The picture shows the tenders stowed on the *Edel Scheel* deck just before sailing.

(*PRDHT*)

1 July 1985. **HMS Ark Royal** arrives in Portsmouth from her builders Swan Hunter Shipbuilders Ltd. She entered flying the Red Ensign, which was lowered during the acceptance ceremony and replaced by the White Ensign. On the flight deck were two aircraft, a Harrier and Swordfish torpedo bomber of the Second World War, representing the future and her heritage. As she came through the mouth of the harbour she was greeted by a flypast of naval aircraft both historical and modern. As the ship glided alongside the jetty, 250 men of the ship's company marched through the Naval Base from **HMS Nelson** to join her. The ship was formally handed over by M A J Marsh, Managing Director of the builders, into the care of her first Commanding Officer, Captain James Weatherall.

(MoD/Crown Copyright)

The date of this picture is thought to be 1985. *Invincible* is on the right alongside South Railway Jetty. Moving left, the white super-structure of the Ice Patrol Ship *Endurance* can be seen astern of *Ark Royal*, at North Corner. *Illustrious* is just above and to the right of *Ark Royal*. *Kent* is moored off Whale Island and just below her is the Royal Yacht *Britannia* in the Pocket. In the top right of picture in No 3 Basin is *Hermes* with possibly *Fearless* and *Eskimo*.

(MoD/Crown Copyright)

1986. **HMS Kent** recommissions. In 1980 she became a harbour training ship moored in Fountain Lake off Whale Island until 1993 when she was replaced in that role by **HMS Bristol**. After languishing in the yard for a few years she was towed away for scrapping in 1997. The picture shows the recommissioning ceremony on the flight deck as the White Ensign is about to be hoisted.

(PRDHT)

May 1986. ***RFA Pearleaf*** leaves harbour for the last time. She was launched in October 1959 and during her service carried out fuel freighting and fleet replenishment duties in all parts of the world. During the Falklands War she left Portsmouth at the same time as the carriers ***Hermes*** and ***Invincible***. While in the Falklands area she achieved probably the longest single replenishment at sea on record, 52 hours and 40 minutes with the BP tanker ***British Tamar***.

(*PRDHT*)

With the decommissioning of **HMS Vernon** in 1986, No 2 Basin of the Dockyard became home to the mine warfare vessels. This picture taken in 1986 shows **Wotton** (M1195), **Hubberston** (M1147) and **Kirkliston** (M1157) moored in No 2 Basin. The ship on the inside of **Kirkliston** is unknown. The long building in the background was built in 1848 as a steam factory for the repair and manufacture of steam engines. No 7 Dry Dock can be seen at the stern of **Wotton** and has since been filled in, along with No 10 Dock at its other end. Both now form a car park.

(PRDHT)

In the early part of 1986 **Illustrious** suffered massive gearbox explosion and fire in her forward gear room. The gear-box, whose size was close to that of a small house, was completely wrecked. Repairs took 14 weeks during which the Dockyard rebuilt the gear-box and refitted compartments damaged by the fire. The picture shows fitters cleaning the gearing before the gear-box was rebuilt. The hangar was virtually turned into a mechanical workshop.

(PRDHT)

16 June 1987. **HMS Warrior** 1860 entering Portsmouth Harbour after restoration amid a fleet of ships and boats and thousands of onlookers lining the seafront. When built, **Warrior** and her sister **Black Prince** were the largest, fastest and most powerful warships afloat. She commissioned at Portsmouth in 1861. In 1904 she became part of **HMS Vernon's** torpedo school until the shore establishment opened in 1924, when she was converted to a pontoon, **C77**, for the oil pier at Pembroke. Realising her potential, the Ship Preservation Trust (now Warrior Preservation Trust) was formed. In 1979 the Trust moved her to Hartlepool for restoration. Along with **HMS Victory** and **Mary Rose**, she now forms one of the jewels in the crown of Portsmouth's Old Historic Dockyard. *(PRDHT)*

HMS *Londonderry* passing through the mouth of the harbour. She was one of the Rothesay class anti-submarine frigates built between 1956-61 by Samuel White of Cowes. From November 1975 to October 1979 she was reconstructed to serve as a trials ship for the Admiralty Surface Weapons Establishment (ASWE). This work involved removing her 4.5-inch guns and hangar, altering her underwater propulsion system to water jets for quietness, and stepping a large mizzen mast to carry the new Type 1030 STIR radar. She also undertook trials with the 30mm Naval Rarden gun. ***Londonderry*** was sunk as a target in 1989.

(*PRDHT*)

13 December 1988. The sad entry of **Southampton** into Portsmouth Harbour. During September 1988, while on escort duties in the Persian Gulf, she was in collision with the merchant ship **Torbay**. Damage resulted in the Sea Dart magazine flooding and the loss of approx £25 million worth of Sea Dart missiles. The port side of the bridge structure was crushed almost beyond recognition and there was damage to the Sea Dart missile launcher and the 4.5-inch turret. She was refitted at Swan Hunters on Tyneside where repairs took until May 1991.

(PRDHT)

1990. A unique picture of four Type 42 destroyers occupying all the docks on the southern side of No 3 Basin. On the left in No 12 Dry Dock is *Exeter*. In No 13 Dry Dock is the stretched version of the class, *Manchester*. This dock has since been filled in and its surface area occupied by Vosper Thorneycroft's ship hall, where units of the new Type 45 destroyers are being built. No 14 Dry Dock, the largest of the four, is occupied by *Nottingham* and on the right of the picture in No15 Dry Dock is *Newcastle*. *(MoD/Crown Copyright)*

April 1991. **HMS Otus** returns to Portsmouth having been away for a seven-month tour of duty. She flies a paying-off pennant and a 'Jolly Roger' to mark her final operational deployment after 28 years' service. Sailors from the submarine base **HMS Dolphin** cheered ship when she entered.
(*PRDHT*)

1991. **HMS Gloucester** returns from the Gulf. The Secretary of State for Defence, Tom King, visited Portsmouth to welcome her home and to congratulate the crew for an outstanding contribution to the Allied victory and the liberation of Kuwait. **HMS Gloucester** is a stretched Type 42 destroyer. During the Gulf War she provided air defence to the coalition Naval ships in the Gulf where she successfully downed an Iraqi Silkworm missile with her Sea Dart missile system and also accounted for the destruction of several Iraqi patrol boats by her Lynx helicopters using Sea Skua missiles.

(*PRDHT*)

The new ice patrol ship *Endurance* refitting in C Lock 1992. Built by Ulstein-Hatloand and completed in 1990 under the name *MV Polar Circle*, she was chartered for seven months in 1991 by MoD(N) and made her entry into Portsmouth escorted by Lynx helicopters from *Endurance*. She berthed in the Tidal Basin alongside *Endurance* and was renamed *HMS Polar Circle*. She was purchased outright by MoD(N) in October 1992 and renamed *Endurance* with the old ship's pennant number A171. *(PRDHT)*

The burnt-out hulk of the trial ship ***Colonel Templer*** dry docking in No 11 Dock. While berthed at Hull she caught fire and capsized during the fire-fighting operation. She was salvaged and towed to Portsmouth in 1991. Virtually all compartments except the engine room were destroyed. The heat of the fire had fractured and distorted so much of the structure that the task became a major re-building project. All machinery had to be removed and the ship completely rewired with over 12 miles of cable. All work had to be carried out to Lloyds DTI standards which were vastly different from MoD(N) standards. She completed July in 1992.

(PRDHT)

Looking west over C and D Locks, 1992. bNearest the camera is **_Endurance_** refitting in C Lock. The large fleet tanker in D Lock is **_RFA Olna_**. In the Pocket on the right of picture is the broad-beam Leander class frigate **_Hermione_** with two River class minesweepers ahead of her. **_Ark Royal_** is on the outer wall in the right hand corner of picture. Just out of camera is another Leander class frigate and what appears to be an "O" class submarine with a Type 42 destroyer in the top left of the picture. (*PRDHT*)

Looking north over No 3 Basin c.1992. In the bottom of the picture is the Royal Yacht **Britannia** with **Charybdis** alongside the Promontory. She was expended as a target on 12 June 1993. **Intrepid** is on the other side. The diving vessel **Challenger** is opposite **Intrepid**. She was sold and left Portsmouth on 20 January 1994. Inside of her along the wall is **Bristol**. Other ships are unknown but clearly recognisable is **Kent** moored off Whale Island and **Ark Royal** at the top of the picture with possibly **RFA Olna** in D Lock with **Hermione** in the Pocket above the bows of **Olna**.

(*MoD/Crown Copyright*)

The Aviation Training Ship **RFA Argus** berthed at South Railway Jetty. Originally **Contender Bezant** built in 1981, she was one of the STUFT (Ships Taken Up From Trade) vessels for service in the Falklands Conflict carrying replacement aircraft. She was purchased by the MoD(N) in 1984 at a cost of £13 million for conversion to an aviation training ship to replace **RFA Engadine**. She was converted in October 1990 to operate in a secondary role as a Primary Casualty Receiving Ship for service in the Gulf. With a displacement 28,081 tons and dimensions of 175m x 30m x 8m, she can accommodate six Sea King/Merlin Helicopters and 12 Harriers can be carried in a 'ferry role'. *(Author's Collection)*

July 1993. ***RFA Fort Victoria*** moored on the eastern wall of No 3 Basin. She arrived from her builders, Harland & Wolff Ltd, in April for additional work. Officially classed as Auxiliary Oiler Replenishment Ships, she and her sister ship ***Fort George*** were the first of the 'one-stop' supply ships designed to carry and supply armaments, spares, fuel and provisions. She can operate five Sea King or three Merlin helicopters. With a displacement of 31,500 tons on a length of 204 metres, these vessels rank among the largest in RN/RFA service.

(Author's Collection)

HMS Fearless in No 14 Dry Dock 1993. Few people ever see the old lady exposed like this, in an almost indecent pose, showing her bottom. The staging has been removed and the last of the anti-foul paint is in a cage waiting to be lifted out of the dock. Her bilge shoring and after-cut shore at the stern have yet to be removed and a rating in the cherry-picker is knocking out the last of the bungs, so it is only a matter of hours before the waters rush into the dock and she gains her natural element. About this time the diver search lines that are painted on the bottom of ships started to change from white to black.

(*PRDHT*)

143

11 October 1993. **HMS Spartan** being warped into C Lock from the Tidal Basin. **Spartan** was docked down in C Lock to enable work to be carried out on a defect in one of her sonars. She sailed after undocking on 13 October.

(*PRDHT*)

The Type 23 frigate **Westminster** in D Lock shortly after acceptance into service 1994. Stealth features were built into the Type 23 design to enhance survivability in surface warfare. Part of this can be seen in the sloping superstructure and the elimination of radar-reflecting corners. It is claimed that the stealth features of the Dukes make them invisible to the vast range of anti-ship missiles. They are also said to be the quietest ASW ships in the world.

(*PRDHT*)

September 1996. The Type 42 destroyer *Manchester* is moored along side the eastern wall of No 3 Basin having her 4.5-inch gun replaced. *Manchester* is a Batch 3 version of the class, normally referred to as the stretched version. To improve stability and range in the Batch 3 ships their beam was increased by 2ft, and their length by 42ft which gave them a more rakish style than the rest of the class. The additional length caused some flexing difficulties in the hull which was countered by deck edge stiffening in the form of a D-shaped rubbing strake that also added to their handsome appearance.

(*PRDHT*)

March 1997. The 13,300-ton survey ship ***Scott*** came straight from her builders (Appledore Shipyard), to Portsmouth on 13 March 1997 and was dry docked in No 15 Dry Dock for underwater work to be completed. She was commissioned later that year. The small black cross in a circle painted on the ship's side indicates submerged side propellers (bow thrusters) which are used for manoeuvring.

(PRDHT)

22 November 1997. The Royal Yacht *Britannia* enters Portsmouth for the last time escorted by *Southampton* with the Commander-in-Chief Fleet embarked. From 20 October to 2 November she circumnavigated Britain for her last tour. *Britannia* had steamed 1.1 million miles, the equivalent of circumnavigating the world every year throughout her 44 years service, visiting 1,500 different ports. Her demise ended a line of 83 Royal Yachts over a period of some 330 years. She was one of the finest advertisements we ever had for the country and Royal Navy.

(MoD/Crown Copyright)

North Corner. This part of the yard dates to the first Victorian Extension (1845) when it was the north end of the yard. During the second Victorian Extension (1864) the yard almost trebled in size, pushing northwards into the harbour, but the old name stuck. Between the two cranes on the left of picture were the great building slips, which built some of the world's largest warships. The battleship *Inflexible*, the first ship to be lit by electricity, was launched there in 1876. During the Dreadnought period in 1905-16 all the lead ships of the of the battleship classes such as ***Dreadnought***, ***St Vincent***, ***Bellerophon***, ***King George V***, ***Iron Duke***, ***Queen Elizabeth*** and ***Royal Sovereign*** were built there. Now the slipway site is a car park without a stone to mark its grave. With a tear in my eye, I leave the ships in the picture to the ship buffs and their magnifying glasses.

(MoD/Crown Copyright)

May 1998. Looking west over the northern part of the dockyard with all the Royal Navy's flat tops together. Starting at the Round Tower in the bottom left of picture is *Intrepid* alongside the Promontory, with *Ark Royal* laid-up in the Basin. On the outer wall between the two Type 23 frigates is the *Argus* with the Dutch landing ship *HMNLS Rotterdam* just around the corner. *Invincible* is in D Lock with *Ocean* next door in C Lock. *Endurance* is alongside the south wall of the Tidal Basin. The inner basin (No 2 Basin) is occupied by four GRP minesweepers. A Type 42 destroyer and a Type 23 frigate are with *Illustrious* at North Corner.

(*MoD/Crown Copyright*)

Index